Glenn Webbe

THE GLOVES ARE OFF

*For the girls in my life, my amazing wife Sally
and beautiful daughters Lily and Marcy, as well as my parents,
Huw and Islyn, who gave me this life to live*

Glenn Webbe

THE GLOVES ARE OFF

WITH GERAINT THOMAS

y Lolfa

First impression: 2019

The publishers wish to acknowledge the support of the Books Council of Wales

Cover photograph: Getty Images
Cover design: Y Lolfa

ISBN: 978-1-912631-15-5

Published and printed in Wales
on paper from well-maintained forests by
Y Lolfa Cyf., Talybont, Ceredigion SY24 5HE
website www.ylolfa.com
e-mail ylolfa@ylolfa.com
tel 01970 832 304
fax 832 782

Foreword

As a boy growing up in Bridgend during the mid-Seventies, I regularly took my place alongside the thousands of supporters who stood on the Brewery Field terraces each week to cheer on our hometown heroes. I was even there to witness the infamous New Zealand game in 1978 when JPR was forced to leave the field bloodied by an All Black boot.

In particular, I always watched and admired the wingers who wore the blue and white jersey. During that time, Bridgend RFC were blessed with an abundance of talented back three players and, in particular, quality wingers. Even today the names just roll off the tip of my tongue: Mark Titley, Viv Jenkins, Ffrangcon Owen, Tony Lewis, Richard Diplock and a certain Glenn Webbe.

The wings are the glamour boys of any rugby team. For them, the game is all about the glory of scoring the winning try, having the pace to leave defenders trailing in their wake or simply the ability to be in the right place at the right time to walk a try in.

Glenn Webbe was one of those players who had the power, pace and the natural ability to beat any defender on his day. His try-scoring record speaks for itself – he is still the second highest try-scorer for Bridgend in the Welsh Premiership (only beaten by Gareth Thomas, who played more league games) and is top of the club's all-time touchdown list with nearly 300 tries.

As an avid Bridgend supporter, you could only marvel at the countless tries that Glenn scored for the club. Whether it was just a walk-in or a breathtaking try from 40 or 50 yards, which usually involved a step to the inside before waltzing around his opposite number as though he wasn't there, he was pure class.

His talent certainly did not go unrecognised and he was selected by the Big Five to go on the Wales tour to the South Seas in 1986, where he made his debut against Tonga. Glenn went on to gain ten caps for his country and bagged a memorable three tries against Tonga in the 1987 Rugby World Cup, where Wales finished third.

When I started my Bridgend career in 1988, I couldn't believe that I was playing alongside players who I had watched from the infamous shed at the Brewery Field.

At the start of my career, Glenn always encouraged me – and any other young player for that matter – to go out and play on my own terms and back my ability. He was certainly very supportive and made me feel very much part of the team. However, if stares could kill, I would not be here today, as during one game against Pontypool, I mistimed a kick and chipped it over Glenn's head for his opposite number to score. He wasn't very happy to say the least!

During the early Nineties, sevens was hugely popular during the summer months amongst players wanting to get fit for the 15-a-side format and Glenn started up an invitational sevens team called The Welshmen. He would select players from all over Welsh rugby to play in tournaments across the UK. He was the coach, team manager, selector and often took to the field and showed us how it was done. He was also the paymaster when there was prize money at stake and we did win a few quid on more than one occasion. His motto for the players who donned the red and white jersey will always live with me – it was FAFFA, but I will leave it up to Glenn to explain the meaning of that particular acronym!

Glenn was brilliant at running The Welshmen, and I believe he played a huge role in exposing young talent to the game of sevens. He was certainly instrumental in my development as a player and gave me the opportunity to play in top tournaments throughout the UK. I am certain the likes of Gareth Thomas, Dafydd James and Matthew Lewis would agree. Everyone had a huge amount of respect for Glenn on the sevens circuit, and when he asked you to play, you knew you were going to be part of a winning team. He was a smart and intelligent selector who knew how to set up a sevens team. People underestimated Glenn at their peril, as during his time on the circuit we beat many invitational and world-class sevens teams, including the mighty Fiji at the World Sevens hosted by Abertillery. I think it was the only time Fiji lost in a sevens tournament during the early Nineties!

Glenn finally retired from playing in 1996 and I was fortunate enough to play in his last ever game wearing the famous blue and white jersey, although I don't think it really sank in until summer training for the following season just how much his presence around the club would be missed.

It is worth noting that one of Glenn's endearing qualities was his loyalty to Bridgend: 15 years and over 400 games of loyalty to be exact. It is not often in either the amateur or professional game that you come across an individual who has only played for one club. Glenn wasn't nomadic; his dedication and commitment to the one club, which he loved and where he became a huge personality on and off the field, showed how much he valued and enjoyed playing for his 'home' club.

Off the field, Glenn always enjoyed the craic, either at the Brewery Field clubhouse or on our journey home, calling in at a convenient pub off the M4. Webby was in his element, whether it was playing silly drinking games (fizz-buzz comes to mind) or taking on a random local stranger in an arm wrestle, he was always up for a challenge. He never took himself seriously and always wanted to be on the table which laughed the most. If he wasn't, that would certainly change in the next five minutes, as he would encourage everyone to laugh louder! And, at some stage, there would always be a song to sing and Glenn would never disappoint, with a rendition of his favourite karaoke track – 'Mack the Knife'. And typical of Webby, he was very good at singing as well!

Glenn, it was an absolute honour to play with you and I will never forget the significant impact you made with The Welshmen, not only on the landscape of Welsh rugby but in influencing many future Welsh international selections.

Robert Howley
Bridgend, Wales and British & Irish Lions

Preface

DESPITE THE TITLE, this isn't a book about boxing, although I did do a bit in the ring in my younger days and, once, during one memorable rugby match against Maesteg.

'The gloves are off' is a phrase that suggests you don't hold anything back and this is my story as I remember it with nothing held back – OK, I have had to hold a little back but only to protect the innocent!

Being a Bridgend player throughout my rugby career the book was going to be called 'The Raven's Wing', as a raven forms the club's badge on the jersey, and, well, I played on the wing, so it was kind of clever. But the Ravens were the second-string side back when I played, so it wasn't really right.

There is another reason for the title *The Gloves Are Off*, as I was known to wear gloves to play rugby now and then. As my youngest daughter, Marcy, said, "Yeah, I like it because you were 'Glenn the gloves'." How she knew that I don't know because she wasn't born until after I had retired.

Why did I wear gloves? Well my good mate David Bishop will tell you that it was his idea because my handling was sometimes a bit suspect but that's not true – I wore gloves for the same reason most of you do, to keep my hands warm; it's cold out there on the wing, especially without the ball. I will explain the full story inside.

I just want to say thanks for buying my book – I'm flattered that anyone remembers me let alone wants to read about my life and rugby career but, then again, I played during an era that was filled with larger-than-life characters who got up to all sorts of mischief, and I was persuaded that it would be a good read. Plus, I wanted the money.

I hope you enjoy the read.

PS: If you want to buy a kitchen, get in touch.

Contents

CHAPTER 1

Sisters, school and singing!

IF YOU WANT to know where my speed came from, it's more than likely a family thing – when you grow up having seven sisters you have to be pretty quick on your feet to get to the bathroom first each morning! While I'm known for my sense of humour, that's the honest truth. I was one of eight children and I have seven sisters; if only women's rugby had been more prominent in the 1970s the Webbe girls could have enjoyed their very own seven-a-side team!

My parents, Islyn Teresa Francis and Hugh Michael Webbe, were part of what has come to be known as the Windrush Generation. They had both grown up on the Caribbean island of St Kitts, which is an abbreviation of St Christopher Island, in the West Indies, and decided to accept the offer of the British Government to help replenish the country following the Second World War. They came over in the early Fifties on the luxury ocean liner the *Queen Mary* and actually met for the first time while on board the ship. They had grown up on the same tiny little island, they were both from the capital Basseterre, which had a small population of just over 11,000, yet they only ran into one another on the *Queen Mary* – not bad for a first date!

They resettled around London and my father got drafted into the army while my mother worked as a nurse. Once they married they moved down to Cardiff, settling in Penygarn Road in Ely, and looked for work. My father, who had left the army by then, became a foundry worker while my mother carried on nursing and got a job in St David's Hospital.

There has been a fair bit of controversy in the media recently over what has been called the Windrush Scandal and I suppose my only observation would be these people came here in good faith and helped rebuild this country and life was not easy for them – my father said that if he had had the money he would have gone straight home again. He said it was so cold he thought he could see smoke coming out of his mouth, even though he never smoked.

*

I was born in St David's Hospital, in Cowbridge Road, on 21 January 1962 – you could say my mother had me at work! I was christened Glennfield Michael Charles Webbe but was known as Glenn, because it's a hell of a lot easier and, let's face it, even I would rip into me if I went by the name Glennfield! I was a middle child with four older sisters – Paulette, Bernadette and twins Humie and Sondra (the twins count as one pregnancy, placing me bang in the middle!) – and three younger ones – Jacqualine, Avril and Veronica.

Despite being christened Islyn my mother was known to everyone as Lyn but that was down to her thick West Indian accent and confusion rather than a natural shortening of the name. You see, when people asked her name she would say, "Islyn" and people would think she had said, "It's Lyn", and would call her Lyn. She would say, "No, Islyn", and they would say, "I know it's Lyn, you just said!" In the end she just accepted being called Lyn.

My father was known as Mike in rugby circles – he was a very big supporter of mine and went to a hell of a lot of the games – but the family called him Hugh. He was always a happy-go-lucky sort of character and, like my mother, spoke with a thick West Indian accent but also had a stammer. He developed a habit of repeating phrases so people could understand him.

When I was a kid and my friends visited the house, they thought he was speaking in some West Indian language – I used to play along with this and translate for them! They thought I was cool being bilingual and I didn't let on until years later.

He was never a rugby player but he played football while in the army and for Arsenal. He has always enjoyed telling people this but he didn't always add that he was talking about a team back in St Kitts, which was also called Arsenal! He played up front and was very fast by all accounts. We have some great pics of him from back in his playing days and he was a good-looking guy... something else I inherited from him I hear you say! My father was always a fit man and he would walk everywhere, even back and forth to work before he retired at the age of 82! He had a strong work ethic which I guess I inherited. When I was small, I used to race him every day on the walk to school until one day he stopped. That's when I knew that I was getting quicker, when he stopped accepting my challenges on the way to school.

Throughout our schooldays all my sisters were quite prominent athletes, with my youngest sister, Veronica, being particularly sporty – her daughters, Tia and Hallie, have kept the tradition going, through playing netball for Wales. As a rule, people of West Indian heritage are quite athletic. I'm not sure whether it's a genetic thing, but in places like St Kitts, when you have very little to do and the weather is so good, everyone is outdoors. Without realising it, you will be out playing, running around and kicking a ball and having races. Saying that, I wouldn't say my mother was particularly sporty, although when I was in school she did win the mothers' race once or twice on sports day.

One thing I did inherit from my mother was my singing voice. She used to sing in church and it was something she passed on to all her children. It's in the family, we all sing. My sister Jacqualine, who is a professional singer, actually won the television talent show *Stars in Your Eyes* one year and started a choir, while Humie was in a pop band at one point,

15

and my daughter Lily is currently at university doing a degree in music. It's always been in the family.

Sunday mornings, growing up, I would try to get a lie-in but the girls would all be up singing. I'd have to stick my head under the pillow! It was worse than sharing a house with the Osmonds! In the end it was a case of, if you can't beat them, join them! I'd get up and we'd have a little sing-song full of harmonising. Then I would be dragged along to church, all with our best clobber on, where the Webbe family pew more than held its own and would have given *Songs of Praise* a run for its money!

Unfortunately, things weren't always so harmonious between myself and my sisters. Being the only boy in the house, things were often stacked against me, especially as my dad was always out and about. I used to get it from all sides. My mother, who truth be told wasn't happy with my father, probably saw something of him in me and would complain, "You're just like your father!" and I'd get a clip across the ear. And the girls used to gang up on me and tell tales; perhaps they resented the fact that I was the only one to enjoy the luxury of having a bedroom to myself. Whatever the reason, I was always fighting them on my own and felt so hard done by.

Things came to a head when I was in the house on my own one Saturday watching *Grandstand* on the television; my father was working and everyone else was out. It was heaven. But then the twins came home. They took one look at the television and said, "We don't want to watch this, we want to watch the Saturday matinée."

I replied, "I've been watching this and want to see the end."

"We don't want to watch sport, turn it over!" came back the annoying chorus.

"Please!" I begged.

"No!" And they overpowered me and turned the channel over.

I was really angry with this. I knew a little bit about electrics by that age and managed to find the fuse box and turned the power off for the whole house before heading out for the rest of the day. "If I can't watch sport then no one is going to watch anything," I told myself. When I eventually returned home the house was in complete darkness because my mother had no idea how to turn the power back on. I got the hiding of my life. I felt it was completely unfair and decided I wasn't part of the family any longer. We didn't speak unless dialogue was unavoidable. It just got easier and easier not to talk and the stand-off lasted for a very long time.

One thing that made not talking easier was the fact that I was out most of the time, especially during the long summer holidays. As with most people who grew up in the Seventies, I would be outside playing with my friends from dawn to dusk. We'd meet at 9am with our dogs – I had a little corgi/ Jack Russell cross called Bronco – and we'd go to the woods. We'd be out all day long. I can't remember eating at home. I can't really recall what I ate during those days; I don't even remember stealing apples! I'd arrive home at around 9pm, in time to get my hiding because I was out too late, before going to bed. Looking back it seems really weird but they were different times.

*

Ely, to the west of the city, hasn't got the best reputation in the world – there were even riots there in 1991 that made it onto the national news and one of the local characters was recently convicted of killing a seagull with his bare hands because it pinched one of his chips – but it was my home, and when you're a kid you don't see what's around you. Every day is just an adventure.

You hear a lot of excuses for bad behaviour, things like 'he came from a broken home'. I used to hear that term quite often and walking around Ely you would regularly see windows smashed or boarded up, gaps in fences and doors hanging off

17

their hinges. There was never a lot of household maintenance, and that's what I thought they meant by a broken home. I didn't realise they meant that the parents had separated or were divorced!

In reality, the area was deprived but it seems to me now that it was quite an education growing up with such people, getting along with one another and making do with what little we had; it made you grateful for whatever it was. Making do and taking care of what you've got. As kids you knew no different, it was always a struggle without realising you were struggling.

Money was definitely tight, coming from such a large family, and I sometimes relied upon hand-me-downs. Now while, thankfully, I never had to wear my sisters' dresses, there was a pair of shoes that ended up in my possession and caused me a bit of grief. They were red, green and blue platform shoes and I quite liked them – remember this was the age of glam rock, and the likes of the Bay City Rollers and Elton John were cool. My mother had bought these shoes for one of my sisters but she fobbed them off on me and I quite literally took a shine to them and wore them proudly to school. They really went well with my flared trousers. I was the coolest boy in school for a short while until one day, while we were changing after gym, a friend called Phillip Pates picked up one of my shoes to look at them and inside, just within sight, were the words Modern Girl written on a label!

"Look at this!" he cried. I was so embarrassed.

"Please Phil, don't tell anyone about this," I begged.

"I won't say anything at all," he assured me, but he really wound me up. There was a song out at the time by Eddie Holman called 'Lonely Girl' and he used to sing it to me on the sly, "Hey there modern girl..."

I'd whisper, "Pates shut up!" and he would just laugh to himself while everyone would ask, "What's he on about?" Thankfully he never did tell.

*

As for my education, I started off going to Herbert Thompson Primary School before graduating to Glan Ely High School. I loved my schooldays and the friends I made there. It was while at primary school that I began to realise that I had a bit of pace about me. I loved running and used to run back and forth to school so I could pocket the bus fare – my mother gave me money for the bus but I would run the three or four miles and keep the money to buy sweets and stuff.

Like all kids at that age we would play various games of chase in the playground at break times and anytime I was not the one doing the chasing, the end-of-play bell would go before I got caught. However, I began to notice that there were a few boys who weren't as quick as me but were very good at dodging. They were like young Shane Williamses and appeared to have more fun avoiding people than I did through just running away. After that I used to practise dodging as I was running along the street. If I saw any litter, Coke cans or cigarette butts on the pavement, I would run in and out and dodge them, even any people who I encountered walking along. That's probably where I learned to sort of swerve. I've never had a fantastic sidestep but I could turn defenders inside out with a subtle change of direction and shimmy of the hips.

It was the same after school, while we were out playing. There used to be a circuit where we lived, down a little gully and around some side streets, that we used to race each other around. I used to throw down a challenge to anybody; one would go one way and the other the other way and the first back to the start was the winner. It was nearly 400 metres all the way around and I always came back first.

I never really got involved in athletics, but later on I did go along to Cardiff Athletic Club for a while when I was starting out on my first-class rugby career, and did a spot of sprinting – I think my best time for the 100m was 10.8 seconds. As for team sports I used to play a little bit of football but I was never really skilful enough on the ball to be any good and it was always rugby for me. I didn't have my own rugby ball as a kid – in school we used to play with a big leather ball with a laced-up valve that was like a bar of soap when it got wet – and it wasn't really a game that you could play in the street like football. You can't really take someone down onto concrete, so it was only played at school.

We also played a fair bit of baseball – it may be a surprise to some people but the sport is big in Cardiff and played in the schools. Our home in Penygarn Road was part of a cul-de-sac, and the bottom end was like a bullring – it was huge. We would play baseball using the lamp-posts as bases and I would glide between them. I still go back from time to time and it's such a small road it's difficult to manoeuvre my car around. It's funny it has this draw; anytime I'm working in or around the area I will drive down and have a look at the old house. I'm tempted sometimes to knock on the door and see if I can have a look inside.

The other thing about primary school is that it provided me with my first inkling that I was any good at rugby, when I was picked for the school team while in Standard 3. You only played rugby when you were in the top class, Standard 4 – there was no tag or junior rugby available to us Ely kids back then – but I was picked a year early. A year is a huge gap when you are kids of that age, and it felt like I was playing against men!

The teacher obviously saw that I had something but, at first, I didn't really see it myself. I thought, 'Why am I playing for the Standard 4 team?'

I can't remember anything about the game but the best thing about it was that I told a few little jokes afterwards and the Standard 4 boys thought I was funny! Little did I know that that was to become quite a theme in my life. It was the humour and the banter that kept me involved in the game and it's been the same ever since I was in school.

*

Anyone who has played representative rugby or aspired to it will be aware that there is always a selection process involved where you have to prove that you're the best. I experienced a selection process of a far different kind during my first week of high school. Now, there were three feeder schools for Glan Ely, namely Hywel Dda, Windsor Clive and my old school, Herbert Thompson, and the toughest kid from each primary school had to fight it out for supremacy, to see who was the hardest.

Although I was small, I was quite tasty and considered to be the hardest from Herbert Thompson School and so was all set to fight in the three-way. Standing in my way were Wayne Wadsworth, from Hywel Dda, who could only be described as an 11-year-old man – he came from a large family of Wadsworths who were all Cardiff City boot boys, all plastered with home-made tattoos – and Barry Davies, who was the hardest kid from Windsor Clive. The Wadsworth brothers had got everyone together at the Ely recreation ground after school; it was a tradition and so practically the whole of the school was there.

The first fight was between Barry and Wayne. The Wadsworth brothers made a big circle and everyone crowded around to watch the two boys slug it out – I'm sure one or two teachers were taking bets from a distance. To be honest with you, the fight must have gone on for half an hour. There was blood, black eyes, split lips, broken noses and their clothes were torn. Eventually they were on the floor and Wayne managed to pin Barry to the ground and he just punched and punched him until, in the end, Barry said, "OK... I give up."

Wayne climbed to his feet, punching the air, and all his brothers started cheering. He then began looking around and said, "Right, who's the hardest kid in Herbert Thompson?" He caught my eye and said, "It's you, isn't it Webbe?"

I just shook my head and said, "I think it's Billy Nichols," and pointed to my friend.

*

We were the only black family in our school and I think there were only three or four other black families in the area while I was growing up. I wasn't really aware of such a thing as racism at the time. To me I certainly wasn't 'different' and all my friends were the same; we were just children. There weren't any racial incidents which would have made me aware that such ignorance existed, until the latter stages of my time in junior school.

That first time I remember one of the kids saying something and I realised, by the teacher's reaction afterwards, that whatever was said must have been wrong, I didn't even know what racism was. I don't know exactly what he called me or what he said but the teacher went absolutely ballistic with this kid, shouting, "You can't say things like that! That's a disgusting thing to say!" I just sat there watching this kid get into such a lot of trouble for just saying something about my colour. I thought, 'OK' and started thinking about the differences.

Then there was another incident, around a month afterwards, when something was said to me out of the earshot of the teacher. I can remember getting sort of excited that I had something important to tell the teacher, that would get this guy into so much trouble. I just felt so powerful. I told the teacher – it was a different teacher – and he said, "Just call him a name back." I felt deflated and thought, 'He didn't get into trouble.' But as it sat with me for a while, I realised that the teacher was right. The right thing for me to do was to think, 'Well he's trying to insult me, trying to hurt my feelings, but it's only a name. It's only words. And I can say anything I like back.' (Verbally, when I was younger, I could give back anything I got and, a lot of the time, I was quick-witted enough to come out on top.) It was at that point that I started to turn things around through diffusing potentially racist situations with humour. That incident armed me with an approach to racists that I have deployed all my life – without a shadow of a doubt, the fact that I'm quite a cool, laid-back kind of guy helps me handle such situations.

When someone is saying something to me, and they are trying to anger me by what they are saying, I think to myself, 'Well, if I don't get angry and if I don't rise to it, there will be a turnaround; I will have all the power.' That makes them miss the target, if you like, because I am not getting upset. I am not biting and they are the one getting frustrated. Such an approach, for me at least, makes me feel more in control of the situation. I think that any time someone says something racist or sexist or ageist or whatever it is, you have the choice whether to be offended by it or not; you have that choice.

It's harder to say offensive things now than it was before, which is obviously a good thing. These days, fuelled by the media in my opinion, to be offended by something has almost become quite trendy. Years ago, people used to say, 'sticks and stones may break my bones but names will never hurt me', but now it's almost a case of, 'sticks and stones will break my bones but names will start a war!' If you say the wrong thing about people it can appear more of a crime than if you'd actually hit someone physically.

*

While I shared my father's happy-go-lucky attitude to life, I suppose my sense of humour came from my schooldays. When I first started getting laughs it was a great feeling. I wasn't stupid – although most of my friends were in lower bands, I was in the top – and I used what intelligence I had to good comic effect. I was always messing around trying to make my friends laugh. For example, I remember our physics teacher, Mr King, talking about Ohm's Law. I quite liked physics and I was listening to what the teacher was saying, but I was also aware that there was some condensation on the window. I began drawing my name and smiley faces on the window with my finger. Mr King stopped talking and I could sense him noticing me but I deliberately carried on and made sure I didn't look at him. He picked up a wooden metre ruler and crept over to where I was and gave my desk an almighty whack!

"Webbe! You haven't listened to a word I've been saying!" he screamed.

"I have sir. I have."

"No you haven't! What's the principle of Ohm's Law?"

"I equals V over R," I replied.

He was stunned and mumbled, "Yes. That's right." The whole class erupted with laughter, just as I knew they would.

Another time we were doing a practical lesson in the lab and the teacher, Miss Phillips, left the room for a short time saying, "I won't be long." I waited at the furthest sink from the door, with the water running, until she came back. I had my back to her, hunched over with my hands down low in front of me, and when she saw me, she cried, "Webbe! What are you doing?" She thought I was having a wee in the sink but when I turned around, I held up a test tube of water!

I enjoyed little things like that, setting traps for the teachers and knowing that they would fall into them. I suppose I was a bit of a smart alec. When I think about it, I really enjoyed school, with all the friendships. There were one or two big characters. I remember a girl called Jane Veysey who brought the whole school out on strike when we were in Form 3. It wasn't really about anything; we just went on strike. There was some dissatisfaction in assembly and she just shouted out, "We're not having this! Everybody out on strike!" Because of the rebellious streak that almost all children have, we all said, "Right, let's go!"

To be fair it was the Seventies, a time when you couldn't turn the news on without seeing some strike or other, so we didn't know any better. Everyone just ran out of the assembly hall into the playground and we started marching around chanting, "We're on strike! We're on strike!"

Another time we played rugby against Whitchurch High School and this wily character, called Paul Ivins, pulled all the signs and posters down from their school hall. Their headteacher thought it must have been one of us Ely lot and contacted our head. Now Paul Ivins was connected, and warned us that Billy Nichols – a big lad, who could handle himself – would beat up anyone who grassed him up. When no one came forward the whole team was assembled in front of the whole school and given six of the best by Mr Winterburn our PE teacher. Now, myself and a few of my friends thought we were clever by putting an exercise book down the back of our pants – the beating still hurt but not as badly as it should have done. Just when we thought we had gotten away with it, Mr Winterburn said, "Now you, you and you, take the books out of your trousers and get ready for the next six." That was a painful lesson in life.

*

I developed a knack for getting into mischief during my childhood. On one occasion during the summer holidays Wayne Wadsworth, Billy Nichols and I came into the possession of three air rifles – I won't explain how, so as to not incriminate anyone. It's hard to believe now but we were walking along the streets with these air rifles slung over our shoulders and pockets full of pellets. It was just a fantastic day of playing war. However, towards the end of the day we were at the recreation ground getting a little bit bored and overconfident and Wayne Wadsworth, who was only joking, pointed his rifle at Billy, who shouted "No!" and grabbed hold of me as a human shield, and the rifle went off! I felt a sudden pain above my mouth. I put my hand up, pulled it away and when I looked at my hand it was covered in blood. The pellet had gone right through my lip and knocked a tooth out and made a hole in my tongue!

When I realised what had happened, I went absolutely nuts. I grabbed my rifle and started loading a pellet, crying my eyes out, and Wayne and Billy ran away across the rec and I just started firing at them – I was like one of those soldiers at

Rorke's Drift! I just kept reloading and firing; fortunately, they both had thick Parka jackets on and neither of them was hurt.

When I went home I was really worried about how I could explain the injury to my mother. I had been warned not to play with Wayne Wadsworth and his gang. This is how young I was; I was still being told off for bouncing on the bed. Luckily my mother was in the garden doing the washing in a tub, so I sneaked upstairs and started bouncing on my bed as loudly as I could and then I started screaming. My mother came running upstairs, shouting, "What's happened?"

I pointed to my mouth and said, "Look! I was bouncing on the bed and fell and my tooth came out!"

"What have I told you about bouncing on that bed?!" She then took me to the doctors and I was tended to. It was only a few years ago, one Christmas, when my sisters said, "Remember the time your tooth came out when you were bouncing on the bed?", that I actually came clean and told them the true story! My mother just said, "I told you not to play with that Wadsworth boy."

*

Only now, having had a family of my own, do I appreciate how hard it must have been for my mother. To be perfectly honest, now that we have labels for this and labels for that, I really think that my mother must have been battling depression. Towards the end of my childhood my father had left – from around the time I was 12 they didn't get along – and it was just my mother trying to cope with us kids virtually on her own. I also now realise why she hardly ever came to watch me play rugby – she was too busy looking after us all.

With all that pressure, there's no wonder she was always saying to me, "You're just like your bloody father!" I never enjoyed being around that misery. She was not often happy but she didn't have a great deal to be happy about; worrying about bills, worrying about money and putting food on the table and clothes on her children's backs. Who wouldn't be depressed? When I was a kid, I would only see things as a kid sees things. I couldn't have this; I couldn't have that. I couldn't go here; I couldn't go there. But I didn't realise why my mother was always miserable, why she was always upset. It must have been one hell of an existence for her. It upsets me now that I didn't realise it at the time.

My mother has passed now and my father, at the time of writing this, is not at all well, so it's quite emotional recalling my childhood and all they did for me. They were always proud of all their children and were there for us in whatever we did without ever pushing us into anything; they just offered their support. And now I'm a father to Lily and Marcy – of whom I am equally proud – I just hope that I am an equally good parent to them. If so, then that's the greatest gift my parents could have given me.

CHAPTER 2

A rugby education

IT WASN'T UNTIL I went to high school that I started playing rugby regularly, but while our PE teachers, Mr Bartley, Mr Smart and Mr Winterburn, were decent enough, we were never the best of teams. We never trained as such, it was just a case of, 'There's a game on Saturday morning, see you there.' We had to find our own way to games – even if it was an away game – relying on a few parents giving us lifts; my father never had a car so I had to look to others for a lift. It may seem an ad hoc arrangement but I used to really enjoy playing rugby in school.

I'm sure there are a few people out there who will be surprised to learn that I actually started off playing outside-half! I was always quick but I wasn't too skilful when it came to footballing ability. However, it was a case of if I was closer to the ball, I could do whatever I wanted to do with it a lot quicker. I quite enjoyed that but, unfortunately, for my hopes of being the next Barry John, I was a bit too greedy and was moved out to the centre, where I was still a bit too greedy, so eventually I was banished to the wing! And that's where I stayed, out of trouble.

Despite our dismal record and a pack of forwards who would be taken apart by a pack of girl guides, I usually manged to get on the score sheet. You see, when the opposition had a penalty and decided to take a kick at goal, it was a chance for me to get the ball! I would stand under the posts and, if it fell short, I would catch it and run as far as I could down field – nine times out of ten, I would run the length of the field and score a try. That was our main move!

When we reached the fifth form, I and some mates, Dennis Paine, Howard Martin and Billy Nichols, started playing youth rugby for Canton – the older brother of one of the boys was already playing for them and we were invited along to make up the numbers. On a Saturday I would play for the school in the morning and for Canton Youth in the afternoon. I just loved playing.

I spent three years playing for Canton Youth and enjoyed every minute of it. In the beginning we were mostly 16 year olds, basically playing against 18-year-old men each week, which was a big difference at that age. Just like the school team, we didn't win many games but it was really enjoyable, because in the clubhouse after games the senior team knew a hell of a lot of dirty rugby songs and drinking games!

It was virtually my step into adulthood, mixing with these guys. It was like, these are men! What's more, they spotted my talent – my singing talent that is. It was a case of "Hey Webbe, you can sing. Give us a song!" I would get up and put my own little stamp on a version of a rugby song. We would sing in the shower; we would sing on the bus and we would sing in the clubhouse; we were always singing.

After the game was always the best time, whatever the result. The fun and the jokes. And when we played away, the coach journey home was always something special and, although I never started off sitting in the back seats, leading the pack, I got there sooner or later!

*

Away from rugby, I left school when I turned 16 with six CSEs. I was never going to be an academic and while I was in the top band in school to start with, my friends weren't and I basically went down and down. My attendance was good, I was always punctual, but I wasn't that interested in learning. As a result, I was always average when it came to reports – except, of course, for PE and Games – and the teachers always said "Glenn has ability but must try harder".

I wasn't lazy or scared of hard work – when I was 15 years old I got a part-time job in a supermarket, after school three days a week, on Cowbridge Road. It was called The International – it must have been a sign! – and was about 100m down the road from Tesco. Today Tesco is still there but The International is a pound bargain shop! I would catch the 4pm bus from school and start work at 4.30pm, work for a couple of hours – stocking shelves and sorting used cardboard in the warehouse – and then I'd go home. It was a very good job for a kid of that age. I would hand over my wages to my mother as I had to pay for my keep when I started earning. It was good to help out as things were tough for my mother with such a large family to keep.

Sadly, my parents had gotten divorced around this time. My mother was always very proud and didn't want anyone to know; she would tell us not to say anything. My father was just a free spirit; he would come and go as he pleased. He stayed with a few friends for a while and ended up with a home down in Cardiff Bay – or the docks, as it was more commonly known.

*

I worked in the supermarket full-time for a while when I left school but then I got an apprenticeship with a firm called Davies & Scott, which specialised in rewinding electrical motors – so you see, I was once a professional wind-up merchant! It was great fun. I really enjoyed being with the tradesmen and all the banter that goes on in the workplace. The wind-ups they used to do – aimed at me as the new kid – made it a fun place to work. I could see what they were up to and turned it to my advantage.

Being the youngest there I had to do all the gofer jobs,

sweep up and make the tea. They used to send me across town for shopping, getting their sandwiches and lunches. And then they would send me out to get things like a sky hook or a skirting board ladder! On one occasion I was sent out to buy a left-handed screwdriver. I went to an ironmongers and started looking around but I couldn't find one anywhere. When I finally asked for help the shop assistant said, "It's a wind-up mate." The penny dropped and I replied, "Ah, right. OK." I thought it was funny but was quick-witted enough to turn it to my advantage and stayed out for another hour just looking around town for something I knew didn't exist. When I finally returned, I told them I couldn't find one. They then put a screwdriver in my left hand and told me to unscrew a screw. Once I had done that they told me to unscrew another with my right hand. They then said, "There, that's the point! You can use the same screwdriver in either hand." But I deliberately refused to understand.

After that they would frequently send me out on impossible shopping trips and I would just take my time and wander around Cardiff, while getting paid! Unfortunately they eventually cottoned on that I wasn't as dim-witted as I tried to make out and the requests stopped, regrettably bringing an end to my leisurely strolls around town

*

My rugby stepped up a level when I was selected to play for Cardiff & District Youth. We used to play on Llandaff Fields and were a decent side – it was nice not to spend a lot of the game looking up at the back of the crossbar and to be on a winning side for once!

We played against Llanelli & District in the final of the Esso Welsh Youth Cup and beat them. The game was played on the Arms Park – it was an amazing experience running out on that ground, especially being a Cardiff boy – and at the time it was the biggest thing to have happened to me. We were a really tight-knit bunch of boys; we were all mates. You would really look forward to getting together with the district, playing, then enjoying some drinking games and a good sing-song afterwards.

Looking back, I was fortunate that my time with the district coincided with several other players who would go on to become household names. Our outside-half was a boy called Mark Ring, who didn't turn out too badly as it happens. Another boy called Adrian Hadley was on the other wing and there was a brilliant flanker by the name of Michael Budd, who was to become one of my dearest friends.

It was only when I was first picked for Cardiff & District Youth that I began to really believe in myself. I looked at these players thinking, 'I remember him, he's a good player' but when you train and play with players at a higher level, and get to talk to them, you realise they aren't immortal, they don't have magic armour. It doesn't dawn on you all of a sudden but it kind of grows on you that you are, at the least, just as good as them.

There were a lot of good players in that side who were, like me, playing for smaller clubs such as St Joseph's, St Illtyd's and Canton. Now the coach of the district side was a guy called Peter Davies – he was also the coach of Cardiff Youth – and he told us that we were too good to be playing for the likes of Canton and we would never play for Welsh Youth because we were playing for smaller clubs. He said that if we wanted an international cap, then we would have to go and play for Cardiff Youth. Ringo (Mark Ring), who was already at Cardiff, also did his best to get us to join him.

I remember getting together in a pub, The Dusty Forge, one night after training with Adrian Hadley and Mike Budd and agreeing that we should be selected on how good we were and not on who we were playing for. We decided to make a pact not to join Cardiff – we all said we were going to stay with our clubs; if we were good enough then it shouldn't matter who we were with. I'm pleased to say that we all managed, eventually, to get capped. I'm very proud of the stance that we took as young men. It was one of the many life lessons that the game of rugby taught us.

*

I had another taste of recognition around this time when I was selected to go on a rugby camp in Aberystwyth for a week. I had been put forward by Canton Youth but the schools also put players forward. I really enjoyed the experience and, at the end of the week, they had a trial game between the schools and the youth, in which I did OK.

The other highlight of that week was meeting Gerald Davies. Now I feel quite ashamed really that growing up, everyone knew a lot more about the game in Wales than me. You see, my father never took me to watch games as a kid so I never really had an idol or any ambition; I just enjoyed the playing, the friendships and the camaraderie. Yet even I had heard of the great Gerald Davies and I actually got to chat with him for a short while. A year later I got some part-time work as a steward on international day at the National Stadium and was tasked with showing former players to their seats. When Gerald walked in, he looked at me and said, "Where am I sitting Webby?" I was really chuffed that he had remembered me – and I'm even prouder that I manged to play on the wing for Wales as he did.

*

In 1980 I was selected by Welsh Youth to tour South Africa, which posed something of a moral dilemma as it was during the height of the country's abhorrent apartheid regime. The British & Irish Lions were touring at the same time – we actually played against the Junior Boks as a curtain-raiser to one of the Test matches – and so the whole ethical dilemma was plastered across the media.

Now, while I never paid attention to the news, I had heard the word apartheid, without knowing too much about it back then, and at the end of the day I decided that I would go and find out for myself. It was also explained to me that I wasn't a politician, I was a sportsperson, and by going there I could probably do more good than harm. To be honest with you, I didn't discuss the matter at all with Welsh Youth – it never came up. As an excited 17 year old, on the verge of representing his country in a sport he loved, I was more or less blind to the politics of the situation. When you are at that age you just think that you are going to live for ever and everything is an adventure.

However, my father started getting a bit of flak when people heard I had accepted the invitation to tour, so much so in fact that at one stage he did actually tell me not to go. Everyone has an opinion and they want to try to persuade others how to think and act, but once I had explained to him why I had made the decision to go, my father was behind me.

Even now, some people ask me what it was like out there in South Africa at that time but the truth is I saw very little to report, based upon the fact that we were ambassadors for Wales and mostly in our own little bubble. We always had our Welsh Youth rugby gear on and so no one was really going to say something or treat us with anything but respect, because we were part of an official tour party. We were sheltered from a lot of it.

That's not to say that on a couple of occasions, when we weren't on official engagements, I didn't hear the odd racist slur. There is one incident that sticks out. I can't remember the exact location – it was somewhere in the Transvaal – but myself and a few of the boys had some free time and decided to enter this restaurant for some food. The place had only just opened for lunch and we were the first ones in there, but, as we sat at our table, those coming in afterwards seemed to be getting served before we were. Having noticed that we were being ignored, one of the boys said, "They're not serving us because of you Glenn." Then someone came over and said that they don't serve black people in that restaurant.

It was certainly the first time something like that had happened to me; I had never been turned away because of the colour of my skin before. It was at that moment that I thought, 'So this is it then. This is what apartheid must be.' I was aware of apartheid, the divide and the racial tension, but that was the first time I had experienced it for myself. I wasn't upset by it, being the type of person I am. I likened it to when you are in a foreign country and try their national dish. Having experienced apartheid for myself I just thought, 'So this is what they are talking about; this is how it feels. No, I don't like it.'

Even when the whole squad returned to the same restaurant, as the official Welsh Youth party the following night, I didn't refuse to go. But while we were there the story happened to come out and when the chairman of the Welsh Youth Rugby Union, Henry Hurley, heard how I had been treated, he went over to 'Mr Rugby' himself, Danie Craven – the infamous president of the South African Rugby Board – and complained. Craven actually made a public announcement and apologised on behalf of the whole South African regime and added that, from that day forwards, the restaurant would allow black people to eat there as well as white.

Henry thanked him and said, "Right, everybody on the bus!" and we all left.

Everyone was so supportive on that tour. I suppose you can say, had I not taken the decision to go on tour, all those players and officials wouldn't have seen at first-hand how archaic the system was in South Africa.

As usual, I didn't let it get to me and saw the opportunity to laugh at apartheid's expense, as it were. When I returned home, the boys down Canton asked, "What was it like in South Africa?"

And I replied, "Well, they talk about racism but I thought they treated me really well: they gave me my own bus to go back and forth to games, I had my own little outhouse behind the hotel and they always made sure I had a table to myself when we were eating."

Years later, in 1989, I was approached to take part in the rebel tour to South Africa – for years the country had been boycotted by international sides in protest over apartheid but the South African Rugby Union were keen to try and break the drought and hired a band of mercenaries. There was a lot of money on the table, £32,000 a head, and quite a few of my friends were on the trip, including my Welsh teammates Robert Jones and Mark Ring – in fact Ringo was able to buy his first house based upon the proceeds from that trip. The pressure placed on my family was far worse this time around. I was a well-known player by then, and I chose not to go. Now people who know me well will find this hard to believe but I turned all that money down!

The fact is, in all seriousness, I had already been to South Africa and experienced first-hand what the situation was out there, so it would have been purely about the money. If I had got it wrong the first time by going there, I now had a chance to make amends. While I'm not one to campaign and make big political statements, I decided on a personal level that it would be wrong to go. I did it out of respect for other people's feelings really – within the black community a lot of people were saying that I was wrong to go the first time and had been disloyal. If anyone had been slighted or wronged, I had a chance to put that right. It was a lot of money to turn down but I had never had a lot of money anyway, so there was nothing new there.

I didn't hold it against my friends for going; I'm not political and I think everyone is entitled to their own opinion and allowed to make up their own minds. I would never try to force my will or my opinions on others – I would state them but it's up to others to decide what they want to do with them.

*

I made a lot of friends on that Welsh Youth tour, including Bleddyn Bowen who was a real class act and would go on to captain Wales when I played, but I didn't hit it off with everyone from the start. In particular, there was a centre called Robbie James, who had been in the Llanelli & District Youth side that we had beaten in the Welsh Youth Cup final – he was their best player to be fair and he was also a good singer and did impressions; I hated him! I really didn't get on with him at all. He was a big-head. After one of the tour games we were on the bus and someone said, "Give us a song Webby", so I got up and sang and afterwards I thought, 'I'd better not sit down or else he's going to get up; Old Big-head'. True enough, as soon as I sat down, he got up and started singing and all the boys from the west were shouting, "Yeah, Robbie, you're the best!"

Then he knew a song that I knew. It was a dirty rugby version of 'Ghost Riders in the Sky', and we both got up and started singing it together, and then alternated verses. That song bridged the whole east versus west, me verses him, divide. We were inseparable after that and since then I have been best man at all his weddings! We even ran a business together for a while.

I really enjoyed the tour. There was a real sense of togetherness and, despite the racist incidents, it was a great experience. I didn't play in the Test match – Phil Ford and Adrian Cambriani were on the wings – but I still had another year of youth rugby and got capped the following year against the old enemy, England.

A Welsh Youth cap was quite an honour back then as Welsh Youth only played against England – sometimes France as well – each season. The game took place in Oxford at the university's ground – so it now says on my CV that I went to Oxford University! When I was told I had been selected I was obviously really happy and excited about playing for my country but some may have thought I was a bit underwhelmed – you see, deep down, I expect disappointment, I expect not to get selected, I fear the worst if you like, so I don't fully let myself go and count my chickens. Until I walked out onto that field, anything could have happened and I couldn't quite believe it until I heard that whistle go. I was like that for a long time, believing I never got out what I put in to things.

Peter Hopkins captained the side from centre and Mark Ring was at outside-half. In the pack were future full internationals Stuart Evans at prop, Terry Shaw in the second row, and Martyn Morris on the flank. Also capped was my good mate Mike Budd. Adrian Hadley, being a year younger, got capped the following year. As for the opposition, I don't think there were any future England stars in their ranks but, as always, they were a big side and we lost narrowly, 13–10.

Back then you could only bring a sub on if a player was genuinely injured, and I pulled a hamstring which meant a mate of mine, Andrew Phillips, came on for the last 15 minutes. While a few people said I went down so he could have a cap, that is not true – I was genuinely injured but he deserved a cap as far as I was concerned.

I don't remember much about after the game, other than we stayed in some hotel and drank more than we should have done, had a good sing-song and made more noise than we should have done!

On the subject of enjoying yourself a bit too much, my father had made the trip up to watch me along with a few of the Canton guys. There's a story that he got so drunk he fell onto the bar and knocked a tray full of pies and pasties on the floor. I never heard the full story but the boys told me I should have seen him. The worse thing was, this happened on the way to the game when they stopped for a few drinks!

*

They say we are all embarrassed by our parents when we are younger – my father was certainly no different. When someone buys you a drink it's accepted that you buy one back later on. When my father used to come to games, people would say, "Mr

Webbe, would you like a drink?" And he would never turn one down but he never really got into the habit of returning the favour. I came out of the changing room into the public bar once and saw that there were four or five pints of Guinness, which was his drink, sitting in front of him. "Who are you drinking with?" I asked.

"There's just me," he replied.

"Whose are all those then?" I asked, pointing to the table.

"Oh, people are just buying me drinks."

I had to tell him that he shouldn't accept a drink if he had a full one already.

"Oh, right," he said.

The next minute someone came up and said, "Mr Webbe, would you like a drink?"

My father looked at me – he had a near full pint – and picked it up and downed it in one and said, "Yes, please." He was a one-off, my old man.

*

Playing youth rugby was the key to it all for me – it laid the foundations for my senior career. I think it is quite sad that, with the way rugby is organised today – with the regions the be-all and end-all and the demise of the schools and youth systems to a large extent – there's grounds for a lot of disappointment at an earlier age. There are only four regions and, if you don't make their academies as a youngster, you face a near impossible task making it. In my day the schools were strong and there were countless district teams to give youngsters a chance. You had all the first-class clubs which held open trial games every season, so the door was always open. Now, if your face doesn't fit or you're a late developer, you can forget it.

The game today seems to be a lot more structured with very little room for individuality. If you get players who are different, maybe they are not big enough or don't comply to the norms, they can fall away. Shane Williams was always said to be too small but he found a way – Neath gave him a chance. I think a lot of players are disillusioned at a young age and are lost to the game.

I think we are producing a stereotype, and players are getting more predictable. It's the difference between traffic lights and roundabouts if you are driving a car – if the traffic light is red you have to wait and wait until it turns green; if you are at a roundabout and you see a gap you go for it. There used to be a lot more flair and individual brilliance.

Today there's so many structures in place, so many analysts saying this should be done here and so on, trying to justify their existence, all wanting their slice of the player. There seems to be about five or six coaches for every player. I don't think that helps. I suppose they see it as producing players who are ready-made for the national side by the time they come out of the academies, but I think they are losing out on natural talent by the whole process – such a rigid coaching structure doesn't allow them to blossom.

Chapter 3

Senior rugby

BEING A CARDIFF boy, I had always wanted to play for my home town club but something happened to change my way of thinking. We were out at the Horse & Groom pub in the city centre, at the end of my final season in youth rugby, and there were a few senior players there, all decked out in their Cardiff Rugby Football Club blazers. We went over to talk to them, as that was our next step, we wanted to play for Cardiff; at that time it was my dream.

I wasn't expecting to hear what they had to say, however. They said, "To be honest with you, Cardiff is a cliquey side, you have no chance of getting in unless you make a name for yourself elsewhere first." Looking back, they were most probably Rags players (Cardiff's second-string side) and more than likely bitter and twisted. Nevertheless, what they had to say did influence me at that time – I did want to join Cardiff but had been disillusioned before I had even tried. I have no way of knowing how I would have been treated if I had given it a shot but it was not to be.

As it happened, Robbie James, who was a year older than me and had become one of my best friends, had joined Bridgend the year before and I thought this might be the step on the ladder to first-class rugby that I needed. I asked him to find out if they would let me train with them. They agreed and I was invited along to pre-season training over the summer of 1981.

Being just a kid really, having just come out of youth rugby, training was definitely hard and a lot tougher than what I was used to. I was up against men who were internationals or just one step down from international rugby. It was more technical than I was used to, there were a lot more moves and calls and a lot more discipline.

Saying that, I really enjoyed training with Bridgend that summer. Towards the end of the sessions we would do striders up and down the field. Starting on the try-line we would sprint to the 25-yard line, as it was then, and back before going up the ladder to the halfway, then the furthest 25 and ending with the full pitch. I thought I was fit but I remember Gareth Williams, or Sam as he was known to everyone, with his white Bridgend shorts, tanned legs and long, rangy running style, just blowing everyone away.

Sam had played for the British & Irish Lions on the South African tour in 1980 – I remember talking to him when Welsh Youth played the curtain-raiser before one of the Tests – and would go on to play for Wales. He was the older brother of Owain Williams, another fine athlete and talented rugby player who also served Bridgend well.

Sadly we said goodbye to Sam in 2018 after he lost his brave battle with Multiple System Atrophy (MSA). It was heartbreaking to see how the cruel illness could defeat such an amazing athlete and sportsman, but he bore it with all the class and dignity that defined him as a person. It was such a sad day for his family and friends, Bridgend Rugby Club and rugby in general, when we marked his passing.

*

The Bridgend coach at the time, Billy Griffiths, must have seen something in me as I was picked to play in the first game of the season against Glamorgan County. I scored four tries and they must have been impressed as I kept my place for the second game, against Cross Keys, and scored a hat-trick. It was long before regions, or even a national league, but there was a sort of unofficial premier league of around 15 first-class Welsh clubs called the Whitbread Merit Table and Bridgend were always one of the top teams. Outside this there were the so-called friendlies against the English sides and, most importantly, the Welsh Cup – known as the Schweppes Cup at the time.

We used to play against London Saracens, as they used to be called, Coventry, London Welsh, Harlequins, Moseley, Bristol, Bath and Gloucester. The matches always drew good crowds, especially the Gloucester and Bath games. Saracens used to play on a park's pitch – you would change in a little wooden shed – and they weren't well supported at all but they have grown a lot since then! They were all good teams but we were a good team at that time as well and usually beat them at home and often away.

Steve Fenwick and JPR Williams had just retired but we had an excellent set of half-backs in Gerald Williams and Gary Pearce and the likes of Mark Titley, Robbie Jones and Howell Davies outside them. Up front we were blessed with internationals and outstanding club players such as British & Irish Lions Ian Stephens and Gareth Williams, club captain Meredydd James, Steve Penry-Ellis and Billy Howe.

Bridgend used to play a nice open, expressive game; we had some really good ball-playing backs and forwards. It was just the Bridgend philosophy – really expansive. You see lots of teams, especially on the international stage, only really trying to open up and run the ball towards the end of games when they are behind but Bridgend's theory was, 'If it's that effective that it can win you a game from being behind, why not play that way from the start to get ahead?'

We trained twice a week, on Tuesday and Thursday evenings, and in all there would be around 60 games a season, played on Saturday afternoons and Wednesday evenings (sometimes Tuesdays). There was a real buzz around rugby and all the Welsh clubs were well supported, especially when there was a derby or a touring side had arrived in town. Like most clubs at the time, Bridgend operated a squad policy where they used to rotate players but, when it came to Cup games, they would pick whoever was performing the best. The other wings in the squad at the time were Ian Davies, Clive Barber and Ffrangcon Owen, while Mark Titley joined halfway through the season. However Ian Davies left not long after I came along and Clive Barber later joined South Wales Police.

*

After home games we would have a few drinks in the clubhouse and then we would hit the town – the big places to go were a bar called The Chateaux and a country club called Crossways. I would usually stay with one of the local boys on the Saturday night and make my way home on the Sunday.

The welcome I had at Bridgend was great. I really liked the people and the simplicity of it all – considering it's only 20 miles down the road from Cardiff it was so much more simplistic – people were warm, welcoming, friendly and direct. They would just come up to you and ask, "Who are you then? What are you doing here?" but in a friendly way.

*

My first really big test came after only six games or so, when Australia arrived as part of their autumn tour of Great Britain and Ireland – for the record the date was Wednesday, 28 October 1981. Now, I used to get butterflies before games at that time but this was another level altogether. We had to be at the ground a couple of hours before kick-off and even at that time the Brewery Field was surrounded by hordes of people just milling around the town. The game was played on a Wednesday afternoon, so most of these people must have taken the day off work to be there. The crowd and the noise were unbelievable. I was just so nervous.

I looked at the programme the other day and it cost 30p – a real bargain even if it does show my age. Our side was Howell

Davies at full-back, me on the right wing, Robbie James and Chris Williams in the centre, Ffrangcon Owen on the left wing and Gary Pearce and Gerald Williams at half-back. The pack was Lyndon Bowen, Colin Hillman and Meredydd James in the front row, Roy Evans and Billy Howe were at lock and Gareth Jones, Steve Penry-Ellis and Sam (Gareth Williams) made up the back row.

As for Australia, the Ella brothers were playing, all three of them – Glen at full-back, Gary in the centre and Mark at outside-half – and I was up against Brendan Moon on the wing.

It wasn't a great day weather-wise but we beat them 12–6, with Gary Pearce kicking all our points. I don't remember much about the game and think that I only touched the ball a couple of times – it wasn't an open game. It was just a case of making the best of the weather; in Australia they don't tend to get the deluges we have, so being a muddy old day suited us more. We had a simple game plan: put the ball up there and live off their mistakes. We had a very good pack and our half-backs controlled it superbly.

I remember being elated after the final whistle. They were an international side. I know they weren't the side back then that they are now but they were still a quality international side. Of course, there was a good old sing-song and a brilliant night afterwards. Best of all, following that game, I felt as though I had established myself on the first-class scene – being selected to play in Bridgend's strongest side against the touring Australians in my first season having just turned 19 years old, was just a massive compliment.

We also defeated Samoa during my time with Bridgend. It was another memorable occasion down at the Brewery Field with one of the best things, in my opinion, our change of jerseys that day! As Samoa wore blue, we reversed the blue and thin white stripes to white jerseys with thin blue stripes – I really liked the look.

*

There was no danger of me getting big-headed after beating Australia, however, as a couple of games later I received a huge wake-up call after being chosen to play against Pontypool. Now, anyone who knows their rugby will know that Pontypool Park, in the early Eighties, on a dirty Tuesday night, was the last place you wanted to go if you didn't have a death wish!

I was guilty of reading my own press and getting carried away as it turned out. While I was quite strong for my size, I was no match for the fearsome Pontypool pack – Graham Price was still playing and I think Charlie Faulkner and Bobby Windsor were also still around, terrorising people, but regardless of what pack they put out, you were advised to update your will before taking to the field.

In those days, if you could keep the ball going into a maul and not let the opposition get it, then you would keep possession for the scrum when the ref blew his whistle. I used to pride myself on the fact that nine times out of ten, if I was caught in possession, I could hold on to the ball long enough to get the put-in to the scrum.

That night I received the ball and ran into a couple of players and managed to stay on my feet in the ensuing maul. I thought to myself, 'There's no way they are going to get this ball off me.' Then I felt someone grab hold of my little finger and peel it backwards. If that wasn't enough, I also felt someone dig their teeth into my arm! At that point I thought, 'If you want the ball that badly, you can have it!'

I never found out who it was nor did I think I wanted to know. It was a case of thinking, 'Wow! Welcome to reality!' There were a few AN Others in our side that night – a lot of people had pulled out and I had wondered why. At least I knew now!

*

The game back then was strictly amateur. In Bridgend we used to have our travelling expenses and a little bit extra – that's what everybody used to do in those days; the little brown envelope. Boot money they used to call it, as you would find a little brown envelope tucked away in the bottom of your rugby boot when you went to change.

I remember towards the end of pre-season training in my first summer. I had yet to play for the club but Bridgend invited me to join their squad for the Snelling Sevens, which was the traditional start of the rugby season in Wales. Although I didn't make it onto the field, it was the first time I was given some boot money. It was great and came in handy as I didn't have a regular job at that point.

Davies & Scott had gone bust but fortunately, after I had signed for Bridgend, the club managed to find me a job with a construction company building the Bridgend industrial estate. We had to start work at 8am but, because I hadn't passed my driving test at that time, I used to get up at 5.30am to get ready and get my sandwiches together, then catch the 303 bus to Bridgend – though, most mornings I would start walking and thumb a lift. I would usually get there by 7am so I would have an hour to wait during which time I would run around the site just to keep warm. We would finish work at 4.30pm and training with Bridgend would start at 6.30pm, so I would walk to the training ground and run around until about 6pm when others would start to arrive and I could go inside. Fortunately, I would get a lift home after training from Robbie or Meredydd James, who both lived in Cardiff. Later in my career, when people made excuses for missing training, saying things like "I couldn't get a lift", I used to think back to my first season and the effort I put in, and shake my head.

*

Money wasn't everything and the fun and camaraderie – as I keep saying – that surrounded the game in the old amateur days was immense and you often hear players saying that they wouldn't swap it for the professional ways of today. In particular I used to really look forward to the away games against English sides – we would alternate home and away fixtures each year – as they were usually stay-aways. We would go up on a coach in time for lunch and plan on a good night afterwards. Despite being so-called friendlies, they were something to savour. I used to pop to the joke shop the week before and pick up things like a swear box – when you pressed it, it would say something highly inappropriate – and fake poo which would turn up anywhere!

Me and Robbie would sit at the back of the coach and churn out well-known rugby songs but we would change the lyrics to create funny versions about the players. One of the favourites was about our captain and scrum-half Gerald Williams, which we sang to the tune of 'Knees Up Mother Brown'.

Whenever he passed the ball away from the scrum he would shout, in a really high-pitched voice, "Ball gone!" He could really screech. So we used to sing:

Oh my, what a rotten song, and what a rotten singer too,
Gerald is our captain, he's Bridgend born and bred
But the shorts that they give him, go above his head
He puts the ball into the scrum,
It doesn't stay there long,
You always know when it comes out because Gerald goes
*   'It's gone!'*

And everyone would scream, "It's gone!" in loud, squeaky, high-pitched voices.

*

I broke several records in that first season playing for Bridgend. I played against Blackwood in the Schweppes Cup and I scored six tries – and I had to go off just after half-time! Then, near the end of the season, I scored eight tries against Forest of Dean in a game arranged at short notice from the fixture pool after our scheduled game had been cancelled. Even then I dropped in two or three try-scoring passes.

It seemed like I was scoring for fun in those days but I also realised that it was easier for me playing rugby for Bridgend than it was for Canton Youth. At Bridgend I was playing with better players, who were all doing their jobs, which made life so much easier for me. They would draw their man and put me into space, do all the dirty work and then make the ball available, and so every time I had the ball, it would be a clear run-in. It was very easy because all the hard work had been done for me. When you play with better players, they tend to make you a better player because they are doing their jobs.

Without being a big-head, while everyone would get excited about me running 30 metres unopposed, I was thinking, 'Well just wait until you see what I can really do!' I was always confident in my ability, which you have to be to be the best.

*

As I was doing well on the field of play I began getting some attention from the press, and while I did enjoy reading about myself there was one occasion that I would rather forget. I was seeing this girl up in Ebbw Vale and she had gone out and left me in the house on my own. I lay around for a while but then I desperately needed to use the toilet. I was sat on the toilet, having done my business and was horrified to see that there was no toilet paper left! Not being able to pull my pants and trousers up, I wobbled down the stairs to see if there was any toilet paper in the downstairs toilet and, just my luck, there was none there either. I then had the thought of using some newspaper – I had seen one on the coffee table – but as I picked it up, I noticed the headline, 'Webb the Wonder Wing: One to Watch for Wales!' Or something along those lines.

'I'm on the back page!' I thought and started reading the story. I was in the middle of a paragraph when the front door opened and my girlfriend's mother walked in, with a bag of shopping, to see me, trousers and pants down by my ankles, reading a newspaper! We just looked at each other for what seemed like ages until I just said, "Err, no toilet paper." I then handed her the newspaper while she handed me a new toilet roll from her shopping bag. Then I just wobbled back up the stairs. The incident was never mentioned again.

*

We played against Cardiff twice in the Whitbread Merit Table in my first season and we beat them both times. I scored a couple of tries against them which was quite satisfying. Although Cardiff never actually turned me down, they were the team that Bridgend always wanted to beat – I think most sides wanted to beat Cardiff. Even if we lost most of our games, if we beat Cardiff then we had a good year and the coach would get another season!

The blue and blacks, however, were to get their revenge in the last game of the season in the Schweppes Cup final. Bridgend had been edged out by Cardiff in the final the previous season and, unfortunately, they were to edge us out again. It was particularly painful because, after a 12–12 draw, Cardiff lifted the trophy on a try count. I didn't make the team – Mark Titley and Ffrangcon Owen were the wings – but I was involved in the squad and sat on the bench. Owen was due to retire at the end of the season and they told me I had time on my side and there would be plenty of other Cup finals (although we had to wait eight years for the next one to come along as it turned out). It was a terrific experience, nevertheless, at a packed National Stadium, and it made me want to play there one day for Wales.

*

While most of the players headed for the beach after the Cup final, I opted for a change of sport – American football. At

50

the time there was a fair bit of interest in the game. It had become available on British television for the first time, and teams started appearing over here. I decided to go along to the Cardiff Tigers, who used to play on Glamorgan Wanderers' ground on Sundays in the summer. I played number one or two running back and I really enjoyed it. Wearing that helmet and all the padding that goes with American football – basically you need the padding to protect yourself from everybody else who wears padding – you feel as if you can run through walls. You just can't feel a thing; you are running through, and you can hear the hits and collisions, but you are untouched. Without any fear of injury or pain you really do run hard.

Rugby is definitely tougher than American football if you ask me. These days there are some elements of American football which are creeping into rugby, especially on the coaching front, with the attack coach and defence coach. Defences now are predominant and most people coach defence drills like never before. Defences are now winning games, unfortunately.

My favourite part of the game was the punt returns, where I used to have the opportunity to run as far and as fast and as hard as I could – it was a bit like being back in my schooldays, when I used to run missed penalty kicks back at the opposition.

I think it helped my rugby. The season after I played American football, I was really running my weight – the only problem was, I started looking for the contact, looking for the collisions, which wasn't my game.

Some people have asked me if I ever thought about playing it professionally, but the team wasn't anywhere near American football professionalism so I had no comparison to determine if I was good enough. I just saw it as a way of keeping fit for rugby.

*

Following that first season I began getting quite a few offers to go elsewhere, including Cardiff, but I was happy at Bridgend. I was even approached by a couple of scouts to see if I wanted to go north and play rugby league. They said that they just wanted to talk but, in those days, it was a big taboo; you could be banned from playing rugby union for such things. There was even a little story in the press that said I had been offered around £30,000 by Warrington. The truth was, we did have a chat but I still had ambitions in union and wanted to see how far I could get and see if I could play for Wales.

I felt that I had made the right choice. I really enjoyed playing for Bridgend and I liked their brand of rugby and I liked the jerseys, they looked good! I had made some great friends and the supporters were really appreciative, plus we were playing good rugby and winning more often than not.

*

Later on in my career I did wonder whether I should join Cardiff or not. I had been at Bridgend for a while; quite a few of the players I had played with and respected had retired or left, and especially when Mike Budd left for the Arms Park there seemed nobody left to impress. Also, nothing was really happening for me internationally, so it crossed my mind. If I was truthful, Bridgend were considered a mid-tier club. You had the likes of Cardiff, Llanelli, Neath, Swansea and Newport, for a while, who were in the top tier, then the likes of Penarth, Glamorgan Wanderers and Maesteg propping up the Whitbread Merit Table, and Bridgend would be in the middle – although we were capable of beating anyone on our day. You only have to look at the likes of Mike Griffiths, Mike Hall, Owain Williams, Rob Howley and Alfie... they all went to Cardiff to further their careers. It wasn't just Cardiff; Brian Thomas approached me about joining Neath – he made the most sense by pointing out that it wasn't so much about the money but about rejuvenating myself.

When I think about it today, I don't know if I wish I had gone somewhere. I suppose it would have been nice to have seen what another club was like but my heart was always in Bridgend. The only time I actually considered leaving was when I was around the age of 28 and I had an offer to sign for Hull. They approached me and I went up and played in a trial game and scored a couple of tries and they wanted to sign me for £80,000. The thing is, I had gone out to Shabby's nightclub in Penarth – I knew the DJ up there – on the previous Friday, it was just after Christmas, and I had met this girl and I suppose she's the reason I didn't go north. I told her that I played rugby and was thinking of going north to play rugby league but I just wanted to see her again.

That girl, Sally, became my wife. We've been together 28 years and she hasn't changed the locks! I used to tell younger players that finding the right club was like finding a wife – you may have to try a few out before settling down! Looking back I was very lucky in that I found the right club and the right woman very early in my career.

CHAPTER 4

Bigots, banter and a banana

SADLY, IT SEEMS racism in sport has reared its ugly head once more, which is quite unbelievable when you stop to consider it's 2019 and we live in a multicultural society. So far, it has been mainly football players who have borne the brunt of it but it's unacceptable in any walk of life. The rugby world, while being far more tolerant, can't be complacent.

A lot of it is media hype – if it wasn't reported then it would be swept under the carpet or ignored, but things like this sell newspapers. It seems like there's more racism now than there ever was, but there's not, it's just being reported more. It's the same with knife crime; it's not a new problem but it's being reported more. The media needs to be more responsible in terms of what it says and how it says it. They are giving certain people a platform which they shouldn't have. These people are faceless through doing things in crowds, that's what they hide behind. They are just cowards who are being given a bit of credence. I think it shouldn't be reported.

You can't control what people really think. You can't change their minds. All this legislation is coming from a good place, they don't want to offend anybody, or make anyone feel inferior to anyone else. I suppose the only way they can do that is by making it law, so, outwardly, people won't break the law but inwardly, that's a different matter.

I have spoken about my experiences in South Africa when I toured with Welsh Youth, and while what happened there was despicable, it wasn't totally unexpected during the height of apartheid.

Fortunately, I witnessed very little racism during my senior rugby career, although there were some incidents which, while perhaps not intentionally racist and meant in good humour, when you stop and consider, could be seen as racist. For example, there is one player, who was senior to me when I first joined Bridgend, who always called me Sooty – he still does when I see him at former players' reunions – and so I used to call him Meredydd, because that's a funny name as well! I know he doesn't mean it as a racist insult but anyone overhearing him, who does not know us, could see it that way.

Another example is quite funny when taken in the context it was meant. Bridgend used to go on a major overseas tour every few years and the season I joined, 1981, they had just come back from Zimbabwe. I remember one of my first games was up in Newbridge in late September, not long after they had returned, and Spike Watkins, one of the biggest characters in the game, was in the home side. We were in the clubhouse after the game and Spike was talking to Gareth Williams and he asked, "How was Zimbabwe, Sam?"

Sam replied, "Yeah, it was great."

Then Spike nodded his head towards me, standing nearby, minding my own business, and said, "I see you brought back a souvenir."

I just looked at him – we later became friends but back then I was only a 19-year-old kid starting his rugby career. You could never get away with saying something like that in this day and age but, at the time, I thought it was really funny. It was just the way Spikey was, he was a really quick-witted character.

Then there was the time I played for Neath – I was invited over to Ireland on tour with them and was never one to turn such trips down – and Brian Thomas's big joke was, "There you are Webby, you won't have to wear a jersey, we'll just paint a white Maltese cross on your chest!" They all roared with laughter at that but I thought, 'I'll let you have that one.' It was quite funny and it was a really good trip. You have got to be able to laugh at yourself, no matter who you are.

A few years back Liam Williams got into trouble for blackening his face, wearing a black wig and going to a fancy-dress party as Swansea City striker Wilfried Bony. There was a public outcry and Williams issued an apology. I wasn't offended by his actions and stole his idea by whitening my face, putting a wig on and a Wales jersey with No. 15 on the back and the question, 'Guess who I am?' on the front!

It was a joke that got a little laugh although I half-expected to have to apologise to Liam but thankfully everyone took it in the right spirit. That's how these things should be treated.

I certainly had a good laugh at this little episode. Bridgend played against Abertillery and on the final whistle all the kids ran onto the field to get autographs. Then this deep, slow voice called out, "Glenn Webbe! Glenn Webbe! Glenn Webbe!" I turned around and there was this guy, who obviously had a learning disability of some kind, holding up an autograph book.

"Yeah, no problems," I said, and I gestured for him to follow me and I took him into the changing rooms and got all the boys to sign his autograph book for him. The following season, when we played the corresponding fixture up in Abertillery, there came this shout again, "Glenn Webbe! Glenn Webbe! Glenn Webbe!" and when I turned around, there was my friend with his autograph book once more. So I signed it again and introduced him to the boys.

Later that season I was asked to play in a charity game, up in Abercynon, and I was in the clubhouse afterwards, chatting to some players and having a few beers, when I heard, "Glenn Webbe? Glenn Webbe! Glenn Webbe! Glenn Webbe!" It was that supporter again. Now I was in the middle of a conversation, so I held my hand up to signal, give me a few minutes, thinking I would speak to him later on.

As it turned out, I forgot to go and see him and, as I was leaving, I heard, "Glenn Webbe! Glenn Webbe! Glenn Webbe!"

Now the bus was about to go, and I shouldn't really have done it, but I just ignored him and carried on. He called "Glenn Webbe, Glenn Webbe, Glenn Webbe," once more but half-heartedly and then, just as I was stepping on the bus, he shouted, "Black b******!"

"What did he just call you then?" asked one of the boys.

"A black b******," I said.

It happened because I had kept him waiting and ignored him. Perhaps the only phrases he could say were "Glenn Webbe" and then, the fundamentally racist, "black b******!" To be honest I just found it quite funny and had to hold back the giggles.

These things happen. If it's not racist, it's sizeist or sexist – there's so many minorities now and there's always someone somewhere ready to take offence.

*

There was only ever one major incident of racism directed towards me during my playing career – although you could argue that was one too many. It took place during my second season with Bridgend, so I was still only a kid really. We had been drawn in the Schweppes Cup against our neighbours, Maesteg, up at the Old Parish ground. It was always a grudge match as it seemed that all the best players in Maesteg ended up coming down the valley to play for Bridgend, while those not quite able to make the grade at the Brewery Field would wander up and play for Maesteg. So they always had a point to prove when they played against us – but we always had that little bit of extra class. All the blood and guts and fire and brimstone came from Maesteg while all the class and expertise, know-how and finesse, came from Bridgend. It was always a battle of styles and always a close-run game, so they would do anything they could to try and unnerve us.

On this particular occasion the ground was packed and there was one hell of an atmosphere. At one point our hooker,

Colin Hillman, was down and receiving treatment so the home crowd concentrated on trying to unnerve us. Playing out on the wing I could hear all sorts – there were monkey chants but I just ignored them and refused to let it affect me. I didn't want them to know that I could hear it.

Then I heard, "Webbe! Webbe! Webbe!" They were trying to get my attention but I pretended not to hear them. Then someone called me by one of my nicknames, "Glenno! Hey Glenno!" I thought that it might have been someone who I knew, so I turned and, with that, a banana came flying out of the crowd and landed right between my feet. I looked at the banana, picked it up, peeled it, took a little bite and threw it back into the crowd – who all clapped and cheered.

It was such a strange thing to do. If it happened today there would be a big police investigation and the perpetrator would face a day in court, there's no doubt about it. But I just chose to think of the bloke who had actually thrown that banana. Did he wake up and say, "Right, what am I going to do today? I know, I'm going to go down to the greengrocers and I'm going to buy a banana, then I'm going to go to the rugby and wait until Glenn Webbe gets near me and then I'm going to throw it at him!"

When you think of the actual effort that he had to go through for something like that – I don't think it happened by chance – he must have been planning it for a week. It was bonkers. I thought of it as a compliment really – if someone had to go that far out of their way, just to get the upper hand, then I must have been some sort of threat. It didn't work either way because, as usual, we won the game.

Gerald Cordle suffered a similar racial slur playing for Cardiff in a Cup match away to Aberavon Quins in 1987 but, I suppose, Gerald and I approach things in a different way because he was off into the crowd trading punches with the bigot in person. That's one way to do it!

*

There have been some excellent black players who have played for Wales since my time, but I would still like to see a few more make the grade. I think the set-up in schools is partly to blame. You can't just go for a little kick about in some corner of the yard like you can with football. If you play rugby on concrete you are going to get hurt. Unless you have actually been introduced to the game as part of your upbringing and you play it in school, then it's a difficult game to get into.

Before I was capped I was asked on a weekly basis by people if I thought I was being overlooked because of the colour of my skin. Obviously, there is no way of determining that but I would hate to think that the Welsh Rugby Union were swayed by the colour of a player's skin, whatever that colour was, and such things were done purely on talent and ability. After all, David Bishop wasn't black, and he was overlooked far worse than I ever was.

CHAPTER 5

Debut

I SUPPOSE YOU could say I have a Tongan prop by the name of Tevita Bloomfield to thank for my first Welsh cap – but I will come to that later.

After four seasons of top-flight rugby with Bridgend, I had firmly established myself as a first-class player and broken all sorts of try-scoring records but it seemed that the Big Five (as the selectors were known back then) still didn't know who I was. It wasn't as if I was difficult to spot out there on the wing as I had a bit of a soul-glo going on with an afro hairstyle and I was wearing my trademark gloves!

I came in for a bit of stick for wearing gloves on the rugby field but to me it was a sensible move as I never liked the cold – I have even worn tights and a vest on the rugby field in my time – and don't forget, there's not a great deal to do out on the wing without the ball.

Not many people know this but our centre, John Apsee, was actually the trendsetter when it came to gloves but he had a medical excuse. Japs, as we called him, was working under his car with a welding iron when there was a bit of a blow back and he burnt his hands and his face. He was in a bad way but thankfully made a good recovery. When he started playing again his doctor advised him to wear weightlifting gloves, while his hands recovered, and they looked pretty cool!

As part of my American football kit I wore special gloves made by a company called Neumann. The leather had been treated so if they got wet it became tacky and helped with my grip. They were phenomenal, especially on wet days. You could practically climb walls with them, like Spiderman! After I saw Japs wearing his gloves, I decided to wear my Neumanns to play rugby because, basically, they kept my hands warm. They were very useful.

A couple of people complained about me wearing them, saying that it was against the ethics of the game. I used to say, so was biting, stamping and gouging but no one was going to go to hospital because I was wearing a pair of gloves. So, I carried on wearing them and they sort of became a trademark in the end. All that fuss brought me to the attention of the manufacturer and this chap from Neumanns approached me and said I could have as many pairs as I liked. They had all different colours but I chose the red. I resisted setting up my own market stall but I did give a few pairs away. There were always kids in the crowd who wanted a signed pair. And I lost count of the number of times people phoned me up and asked if they could have a pair to auction off for charity – so there must be quite a few pairs doing the rounds out there.

*

Despite being overlooked by the Welsh selectors for several seasons, a huge honour came my way when I was selected to play for the Crawshays in the Hong Kong Sevens. At the time there was no World Rugby Sevens circuit like you see today and it certainly wasn't in the Commonwealth or Olympic Games, so the tournament was the biggest thing in world rugby outside playing internationally – it was massive.

We met and trained every Sunday for several weeks in preparation and I had been measured and fully kitted-out for my blazer, shirt and all the Crawshays gear, which I had taken home all excited. It was brilliant. The only little cloud in the sky was I picked up a slight hamstring strain and had to sit out the final training session but I knew that with some rest I would be fine.

Bridgend, however, had a fixture against Swansea at St Helen's the Saturday before we were due to fly out, and I was picked to play despite my hamstring still not being 100 per cent. I told Bridgend that I wasn't quite fit and would rather rest but they said, "Just take your time out there, it will be bad for morale if you pull out of the team." They talked me into playing.

As it turned out, there was this new kid playing for Swansea on the left wing called Arthur Emyr. I didn't know who he was, I'd never heard of him. We kicked the ball down into their 22 and I half limped after it. Now, we had been taught in school to kick for safety when you retrieve the ball back near your own try-line, so that's what I was expecting Arthur to do as I ambled down the field. But this kid tucked the ball under his wrong arm and just went for it! I thought, 'Oh my God, he's really quick!' And so I stretched to catch him and 'Bang!' my hamstring went. He ran the length of the field and scored a try while I lay on the ground clutching my leg in agony.

The next morning the *Western Mail* carried a picture on its back page of Arthur Emyr breezing past me as I desperately tried to reach out to tackle him. And as if to rub salt in my wounds the headline screamed, 'Arthur Emyr Rounds Webbe!'

I didn't go to Hong Kong. Arthur Emyr went in my place. And if that wasn't bad enough, I had to meet him before they left to hand over all the Crawshays kit I had been given. When I told Bridgend what had happened, they said, "Oh well, if you were not fit you shouldn't have played." I was absolutely gutted and I had nobody to blame but myself. I had tried to do the decent thing by Bridgend but I really wanted to go on that trip. That incident really made me realise you have got to look after number one.

*

I was enjoying my rugby and playing a hell of a lot of games. Besides Bridgend, I was a regular for the Crawshays and Glamorgan County and playing an awful lot of sevens in the summer, but I would be lying if I said I didn't start to wonder about international recognition at that stage of my career. I was 24 years old, with four seasons of first-class rugby under my belt playing against the top wings in Wales, week-in, week-out, and, for the most part, getting the better of them but not getting anywhere with the national side. As far as I could see, I wasn't even close as I was even overlooked for the Wales B team (or Wales A as it later became known) which was seen as a stepping stone to full honours.

It reached the point where I decided to turn my back on Wales and play abroad. I had played for Crawshays on a mini tour in France and managed to round the great Serge Blanco when we played against Biarritz. I had been out to France with Crawshays several times and the French would always say to me, "Come out and play in France." And so, when St Gaudinois – they were a second division side but they wanted to pay me! – approached me, I decided to go for it.

People always asked why I hadn't been picked by Wales but there was nothing I could do. I have always said that it is easy to play well for your country if you are good enough but the hard part is getting picked. And I wasn't good at getting picked, or so it seemed. That is why I decided to go and play in France. I honestly thought that my chance was never going to come, so I had better try to make the most of whatever opportunities I could before it was too late.

I had a couple of weeks over there and played a couple of games for them and it was agreed that I would join them at the start of the following season. The package was amazing; they were going to give me my own bar to run – there definitely would have been a karaoke machine in the corner somewhere but I would have hogged the mic!

Ironically it was the WRU who put a stop to me going to France. I was told by the French that I needed a green card – a licence – from the WRU but they wouldn't allow me to have one. When I asked them why not, they said that they were keeping an eye on me and wanted me to be involved in the Welsh set-up. I was half chuffed but also gutted to miss out on my French adventure.

I think I would have really loved life in France; I had a great few weeks over there. I loved the lifestyle and the fact that everything stopped for a couple of hours in the afternoon, no matter what, for a siesta. I remember watching a postman knock on a door and having a good old chat before handing over a letter, then going to the next door and spending another few minutes putting the world to rights. The pace of life was just so leisurely, I think I would have really enjoyed it. I also liked the way they played the game.

*

The WRU were true to their word and I was selected to play in a Welsh trial in 1985. The WRU used to hold trial matches at the start of every international season to help them pick the side. As you can imagine, there were always quite a few players with a point to prove at a time when some said it was harder to be dropped than selected!

I was in the Possibles, wearing white, and lining up against me in the Probables, wearing red, was my old Cardiff & District Youth teammate Adrian Hadley. I scored two tries and the whites beat the reds but I wasn't selected. However, the following November I was picked in the Wales squad for a game in Cardiff against Fiji. I didn't make the team or the bench but I was getting closer and the following season I was chosen for the tour of the South Sea Islands with games against Samoa, Fiji and Tonga.

It was amazing to get the letter informing me I had been selected for the tour. I really wanted to go; it was me, I was right in there! I just felt excited – there weren't any thoughts of being accepted, I just thought to myself, 'Now I'm here I will be able to show what I can do!' I had played with or against most of the players who were there and knew that I was fit – I used to enjoy training and I knew that I was fast and quite strong.

The Welsh coach at that time was Tony Gray and I liked him. He was a north Walian fella and seemed to be very fair. Before the tour they had an evening where you would spend some time just talking to him, his sidekick Derek Quinnell and our tour manager, Clive Rowlands, and it was a chance to make any observations or air any grievances as a player. They brought you into the room, nobody else, just you, and had a little chat – you were outnumbered but at least you were given a chance to voice an opinion. I had never taken part in anything like that before and it really made me feel as though I mattered.

Wales hadn't been on tour much for around 20 years or so, but because the inaugural Rugby World Cup was being held in Australia and New Zealand the following year, the powers that be in the WRU thought they'd take a nice easy trip down to the South Sea Islands as a gentle warm-up. The only problem was, someone forgot to tell the locals that it was supposed to be a nice and easy trip! Although we won our three games, there were more than a few casualties out there.

Now, everyone knows that when it comes to handling skills, the South Sea Islanders are on a different level – you only have to look at Fiji playing sevens, it's like watching a team of conjurers, the things they can do with the ball in hand. It's just something that's ingrained in their DNA, as we discovered on that tour.

I will never forget how, towards the end of a training session, we saw some local kids playing touch rugby. A few of us thought we would do our duty as ambassadors of the game and go over and show them how the Welsh boys play the game – it would be good PR. So we joined in and they ran rings around us! We couldn't get anywhere near them. In the end they said, "We'll just carry on playing on our own over here."

They just have a natural ability with the ball in hand and

every one of them has an electrifying goose-step which just out-foxes everybody. I can see what it is when it's broken down but I just don't understand how they do it. The pace of it, it's almost like a skip or a hop – it just seems to stop time. It's not a sidestep, because they are going in the same direction, but it's enough to throw you off. It's just the restarts of the game that let them down and things like the sneakiness in the tight, although that's getting less prevalent now with TMOs, but that is how we used to wear them down – we would just tie them into a tight game.

I wasn't involved in the first game, a 22–15 win against Fiji, but was picked on the bench in the second against Tonga. Back then there were only two players allowed on the bench, one forward and one back, and you were only allowed onto the field if the player you were replacing was genuinely injured, so at that point my first cap was by no means the certainty it would have been today, when it's as if all seven subs and the coach driver get to go on in the last five minutes! Fortunately for me, however, the Tongan prop, Bloomfield, was intent on making sure there were more walking wounded than returned from Dunkirk!

Bloomfield was a really thick-set guy – we thought our prop Stuart Evans was a big guy but this fella was heavier, wider and probably two inches taller – and his sole intention was to cause mayhem. He was literally going around with his fist cocked ready to take a swing at anything that moved in a Welsh jersey. He wanted to punch lumps out of everybody. We all tried to keep away from him – it was just weird.

At one point he was punching one of the boys and Bleddyn Bowen came running in from behind and hit this prop on the back of the head. He must have thought it was raining or something as he turned around with a look of bemusement on his face. He then looked at Bleddyn and realisation hit home and he started chasing him! Now Bleddyn had second thoughts and started running away and ran straight off the field and into the crowd. I was watching all this from the stand as I was still on the bench. There was a rope around the pitch that was supposed to keep the crowd back, which Bleddyn hurdled like Colin Jackson, but the crowd threw him back out onto the field. This prop was just gunning for Bleddyn.

A little while later Adrian Hadley scored a try under the posts and Bloomfield must have taken it personally as he decked him as he was walking back. Hadley went down like a sack of spuds (to use a polite term) and it all kicked off again. To be honest with you I was just laughing – any player will tell you there's always a little bit of rivalry between two players of the same position, especially from the one sat on the bench! I just thought it was funny and said to myself, 'Oh gosh, look at that!' But then he didn't get up. He wasn't moving!

The next thing I knew, Tudor Jones, our physiotherapist, turned to me and said, "Get your tracksuit off." And it wiped the smile right off my face. I even looked around me to check he was talking to me. When I realised what was about to happen, I thought, 'Oh well, here we go.' That's how I got my first cap, as a replacement for Adrian Hadley who had been knocked out after scoring a try under the posts!

Hadley was taken to hospital – the ambulance actually drove across the field and had to swerve to avoid little pockets of fighting. I think Phil Davies also had to go for treatment. To make matters worse, when they arrived at the hospital everyone there was watching the game on television, so they had to wait to be treated!

The Tongans were big people. I remember observing the cultural difference between the islanders and ourselves: how shy they were off the field of play and how humble they were, not even looking you in the eye when they talked to you. But stick a rugby jersey on them and they were licensed to kill! They were really physical people. They had about four elbows each and six knees. Everything was rigid and pointy with big bones and large heads – they were rock solid. Even the softer parts of their bodies were harder than ours.

Fortunately, I managed to see the game out without having to join the boys in hospital and we won the game, 15–7, despite losing the boxing match by a couple of knockouts! The only Welsh player to win his bout was John Devereux, who gave his opposite number a hiding.

I must have done OK as I was picked to play in the final game of the tour against Samoa, albeit on the left wing – Mark Titley had managed to worm his way onto the right wing – but a cap is a cap I suppose. I had this silly thing about being selected on the right wing. Sometimes I would be picked on the right and end up scoring on the left but I just had this thing about being selected on the right. I had a natural bias. I had a strong left hand-off and a lot of the time I tucked the ball under my right arm and carried with my right so I found it easier. I was right footed and if there was going to be a cross kick, it was always easier for me to chip back infield. I suppose you could say left and right wing is the same as playing tighthead or loosehead prop. They have differences that you get used to, although I suppose you could do both, but I preferred the right wing.

We won again, 32–14, so I was happy enough especially as Titley didn't have a very good game. You always had to have a bit of banter with each other and I remember taking the mick out of him a little bit. There were some kids after autographs after the game. I wrote mine and then asked for another piece of paper and signed 'Mark Titley'. I then told the kid to follow me and we went up to Titley and said, "Hey Mark, this little boy wants to give you your autograph back."

*

My Welsh cap was presented to me by Ray Williams of the WRU at the Player of the Year dinner in Bridgend at the end of the season. My family were there – they all knew about it but it was a complete surprise to me. You only get one cap, no matter how many games you play, which is only natural I suppose as you only have one head! I think it's in Canton Rugby Club now. Then came the official cap photograph. They took it at the Bridgend clubhouse. They sat me down in my jersey, with my arms folded, and I put my cap on top of my afro!

*

You do notice subtle changes once you have been capped. I found that more people knew who I was, there was more pointing going on. "Look. That's that Glenn Webbe bloke." Before being capped people used to come up to me and say, "You should be capped." And after you are capped, they are calling for you to be dropped!

Even your friends change. Acquaintances sort of latch on and make more of the friendship than it was and your close friends seem to step back a little bit and complain, "Oh, he's outgrown us." But I hope that was never the case with me. In fact, after every international I would always want to get back to the Cavalier in Canton and talk about the whole experience with my friends. Perhaps it was a way of me wanting to stay in touch and keep grounded. I still have the same friends today that I had in school – even Wayne Wadsworth!

The only difference was people would listen to what you had to say. You didn't have to fight to get your voice heard. But then you realise that you didn't have a great deal to say in the first place.

*

It's often reported that I was the first black player to play rugby union for Wales – although Mark Brown, the Pontypool flanker, was actually capped before me and he was of mixed heritage. The truth of the matter is, to me, I never saw it as a race thing. I was just a rugby player and like to think I was pretty good at it and so was picked to represent my country. My view of the world hadn't changed since I was a schoolboy encountering ignorance and racism for the first time. We are people who are all the same and should not be defined by the colour of our skin.

CHAPTER 6

The Five Nations

TO PLAY FOR Wales in the South Seas was a tremendous honour and great recognition. I was chuffed to have been capped and I couldn't wait to get home to see everyone and get my congratulations, so to speak, but I really wouldn't be happy until I had played in the Five Nations. It's what you grow up watching and every kid in Wales dreams of running out in front of a packed Arms Park – or Principality Stadium today – especially if you were a Cardiff boy and had grown up with the stadium dominating the skyline. Fortunately, I was given a chance the following season, in the 1987 Five Nations.

I would have to wait to make my home debut though, as our first game was against France at the Parc des Princes. Although it wasn't to be a result to remember – we lost 16–9 to a French team that would go on to complete a Grand Slam – it was an experience I will never forget. The whole trip was just crazy. The best part was the French police getting us to the game from our hotel. I think they deliberately delayed the escort just so they could rush us through the streets of Paris at the last minute, with flashing blue lights and sirens wailing. We got to the stadium on time but the journey was far from leisurely. It was really exciting looking out the widow as we shot through red lights while motorbikes stopped traffic ahead of us. It was amazing – a real adrenaline rush.

Despite the mad dash across Paris we arrived at the ground well before our opponents. The French had a completely different, laid-back approach to the game. I remember seeing them turn up in dribs and drabs, thinking to myself, 'We're playing in less than an hour.'

I was surprised to discover that they seemed to know who I was. I remember reading the programme before the game and they had a little bio on all the players. In my case they said that Glenn enjoys jazz and is a big Michael Jackson fan – I suppose they were referring to my hairstyle which was quite long and frizzled, or perhaps the gloves gave it away! They had basically made things up. I do quite like jazz but they made out that it was all I lived for! I did wonder who they had been speaking to – I wouldn't have put it past Ringo.

When we went out for a stroll around the pitch, about an hour before kick-off, I happened to look up into the stands and saw my father sitting there. I waved but he just turned his head as if to see who I was waving at. When I spoke to him after the game he said, "I saw you on the pitch before the game, who were you waving at?"

I replied, "You of course."

And he said, "You could see me from down there?"

"Well you could see me waving, couldn't you?!"

It was quite funny that he didn't realise it was a two-way thing. I suppose, being part of a crowd, he had a crowd mentality.

As for the game itself, there's not a lot to say other than we were well beaten and could only manage three Paul Thorburn penalties while France scored two tries, a conversion and two penalties. When we got back to the hotel after the game there was a jazz band playing in the reception and they got me up to sing! They were saying, "Oh yes, Webby. Jazz boy!" I guess they had read the programme.

*

Despite the loss in Paris I held my place in the team, which was great, not least because next up it was England in Cardiff!

It was just electric. Before the game you would have everyone getting in touch, not so much to wish you all the best but to ask for any spare tickets! I think even Wadsworth may have looked me up and said, "Hey Webbe, I never gave you a kicking in school so how's about a ticket for the game?"

As a player you would have one or two free tickets and an option to purchase a few more. You also had guys touting for tickets. It was a big business, and still is in some areas. You could get four times the face value so I may have sold the odd ticket here and there – well, I didn't need one for myself!

The anticipation built during the lead-up to the game. We met up as a squad on the Friday and had a last run out and then, in the evening, we were free and decided to go to the cinema in town. I was never one to have a few pints before the game – unlike some – as I was not a big drinker, but a couple of times I did get out of the hotel and walk around town. I was always excited and would look for any chance I had to get out and feed off the crowd. It was just an amazing occasion – you were energised by it all. There was something in the air, it wasn't even a personal thing. You knew that you were a part of something big.

I had to go incognito of course but a few times someone would look at me and say, "You're Glenn Webbe!" And I would say, "No, but everyone says that mate. I wish I had his money!"

I just wanted to have a wander around and listen in to what people were saying and pick up on everybody else's excitement. It was such an amazing feeling and added to the occasion. I always had time for people; it was great, such an occasion.

The night before the game was obviously different because you are not at home and you do have a restless night, but it's more in excited anticipation than nerves. I would try to go through scenarios that might occur during the game – just a bit of visualisation, so if they did happen it would be second nature because I had lived it. I used to do that on a regular basis, even when I was playing for Bridgend.

I would sit in the bath for an hour and think about what could happen – if the ball goes over your head or there is a two-on-one situation in defence, with someone on the outside where you nip it in the bud and hit them before the ball goes out. All these little scenarios which you can think of, then you just live them and dream them. Nine times out of ten one of those situations would happen on the field and it was as though I had done it before. You don't have to react, you can anticipate.

I was up against Rory Underwood. Once, when I came inside, I remember running at him thinking, 'I'm going to step to my left, to drag him infield, and as soon as he comes in, I'm going to step out and go around him.' That was my thought process.

Although the game itself really does fly by, in the blink of an eye, in the actual individual moments, when you are doing something, you seem to have so much time because your instincts are so sharp, real time seems to be slowed down. Everything seems to take an age, even when you are in possession. It is as if you are working in slow motion. You have such an adrenaline rush, such a heightened sense of awareness, you see things slowly. It's almost as if you are not there and you are looking down on yourself. But when I watched it back on television it was a split second. I had the ball and bam, bam, bam, I was past him.

When the time came to make our way to the ground – being based in the Angel Hotel we didn't need a coach – we just walked across the road. Westgate Street was a sea of people and you just made your way through. People would be screaming out your name but you didn't have time to acknowledge anyone.

Once there, it seems incredible today but we never went out to warm up or do any drills. We would just do some stretching in the changing rooms and then a quick one to ten on the spot before going out. I used to take a skipping rope with me so I could have a little skip in the showers. It was only towards the late Nineties that most Welsh sides started having a brief team run on the field. Then, after the game, there was no cooling down. You would start cold, finish cold and then have a cold beer. There was no rehab.

I always sang the national anthem and I know all the words. I remember the design of the Arms Park being a like a bowl, which meant that the sound echoed all the way around and, because of the distance from the crowd, each note seemed to last four times as long. You are all singing in unison but it's one big echo. It's was an amazing stadium, known all over the world.

The media, as usual, had built the game up as England hadn't won in Cardiff for 24 years and they were determined to end that abysmal run but, of course, we didn't want to be the first Welsh side to lose to England in all that time. They always come with a heavy old pack but the fact that you are playing against England is always worth ten points to Wales: it brings out a passion that you don't really have to dig deep for, it's just there.

In the first five minutes there was a bit of pushing and shoving between our second row, Steve Sutton, and theirs, Steve Bainbridge, at the front of the lineout and the referee had to step in to calm things down. Then, when the ball came in, Phil Davies, our No. 8, pushed his opposite number, John Hall, and Wade Dooley – who was their enforcer – came in and hit him with a haymaker from behind. Bill McLaren described the punch as a "tremendous bang" and Phil went down like sack of watermelons (they are bigger than potatoes!) with his cheekbone broken in three places. This was back in the days when you could throw a punch at international level! There were no yellow cards and certainly no TMO, so Dooley stayed on the field. Believe it or not, Dooley was a serving policeman at the time, as was Phil Davies!

I was out on the wing on the other side of the pitch when it all kicked off, so it was nothing to do with me. These sorts of incidents were generally left to the forwards, so I didn't really look across to Underwood and ask if he wanted to mix it up. I

75

wanted to swap jerseys with him afterwards and blood would be a pain to wash out, especially on white! I swapped most of my jerseys but not after my first cap against Tonga, even though it was number 16. I was never going to part with it.

Occasionally a few forwards would try to throw something my way on a rugby field but I seemed to be able to handle myself. Most of these forwards were a bit slow and I was quicker, more nimble and stronger than they realised. There was one occasion, when Bridgend were playing against Maesteg at the Brewery Field, and I scored a really nice try after a planned moved where I came into the line down the left-hand side, beat five or six players, and went under the posts. As I was running back a Maesteg back-rower dropped his shoulder into me and knocked me to the ground. I just saw red. I sprang up and threw him to the floor and rained something like 20 punches into him. Everyone joined in the fun and there was a mass brawl. Once the referee had regained order, I knew that he would target me and I started panicking because we were due to play Neath in the Schweppes Cup final the following week. It was at a time when cards had been brought into the game and, as the referee got closer, his hand reached down to his pocket. I started thinking, 'Please don't send me off! Please don't send me off!'

I just tried to walk as far away as I could while our captain, John Apsee, pleaded with the ref and, in the end, he just brought a yellow card out and I was only sent to the sin bin for ten minutes. I remember sitting there sulking, with someone's brown duffel coat on. To make matters worse, I hadn't long started going out with Sally, and her nan, who was from west Wales, didn't approve of me – she wasn't used to black people and always used to ask whether Sally would be safe with me! The next day the game was on *Rugby Special* and Sally's brother, David, was watching with their gran and he said, "There you are, look. There's Sally's new boyfriend."

"I knew it!" she shrieked.

A few days later, a card came for me through the post

wishing me all the best for the Cup final and it was from the referee! His name was Chris Jones. I ran into him a while later and thanked him, as he did me a massive favour.

I could be the hardest man in world rugby today as you don't have to throw a punch! You just daren't with the TMO and all the eyes that are on you. They just grab jerseys and make faces but that's as far as it's going to go. I can't remember the last time I saw a punch thrown at international level. I'm not saying that punching was a good thing but it was one way of letting off steam. It was the law of the jungle – if you could get away with it, then great.

Although I laugh at the handbags that go on today, I think it's a good thing they don't throw a punch. The reality is, with the game being professional, it could cost a player a lot of money and even their career today. Not to mention the injury element; players today are twice as big – they are in the gym twice a day. If someone really threw a punch, there could be a fatality.

But fighting was part of the game when I played. I used to love sitting down with the forwards and listening to them tell war stories. Things like how they would drop their binding in the scrum and send one through to the opposing second row. All little tricks of the trade that made me happy to be out of the way on the wing.

It even entered the game plans. We were playing against Cardiff at a time when Hemi Taylor was doing great things. He had such a powerful burst from the base of the scrum, a low centre of gravity and was quickly into his stride, so he would take three players with him, and would have been the difference between us losing and winning. Now our hooker, Ian Greenslade, known to all as Compo, had just joined us from Cardiff and was a very shrewd player, who came up with a plan to nullify his former teammate. In a team talk Greenslade told our prop, Paul Edwards, to hold Hemi Taylor down in the ruck.

"But he will hit me," pointed out Edwards.

"Don't worry about it," Greenslade told him, "Just curl up and protect yourself."

Then he told our flanker, David Bryant, "Pull his shirt at the back of the lineout and hold him back." Then he said, "Just leave the rest to me."

So, at a ruck, Edwards grabbed Taylor's ankle and held him back and they ended up fighting. Eddie was just protecting himself and Taylor was throwing all the punches. The referee put a stop to it and told them to shake hands. Then Greenslade told Bryant to step in at the next lineout. Punches were thrown and the referee looked at Taylor and said, "Not you again!"

Soon after, Greenslade took over and the referee blew up and sent Taylor off. It was all strategically done. Cardiff played the rest of the game with 14 men and we won. It was a masterstroke by Greenslade. Who said that forwards were thick?

*

It's not inconceivable that England had planned a mass brawl to try and intimidate us but, if that was the case, it didn't work. As it turned out, we did all right when it all kicked off and I think that was the turning point of the game. England realised that we weren't going to take a backward step – in fact, we took several steps forward and the game turned.

It had rained heavily before the match and so wasn't a day for running rugby, with the game being dominated by penalties. There was only one try scored that day – a one-yarder by our prop Stuart Evans. Says it all, really. To be fair, he had three players on his back crossing that line. Jonathan Davies had switched back to the blind and put up an up-and-under, which I chased, and Marcus Rose wilted under the pressure and spilled the ball before Stuart picked it up and scored.

It was a hell of a game and best of all we won 19–12 and made sure it would be at least a quarter of a century between England wins in Cardiff. It was a tremendous feeling to win – that goes for any win but it was especially so against England. They were always the team to beat and I think that will always be the case.

We had a great night after the game. The two places to go to were this big bar called The Bank in St Mary's Street and then a club called Jacksons later on, but first and foremost was the players' room deep inside the stadium. We boys basically had an hour to ourselves, when we were able to pat ourselves on the back and have a little powwow, reflecting on how things went over a couple of drinks. Today's players are virtually owned by the public – even before they come off the pitch there's a microphone shoved in their face while they are still panting. They get paid for it – but they are not their own man.

You are still on a high – it doesn't go once the game is over, it just changes shape and direction. Even if you have lost, that hour is so important – it's just you, the team, and that is all that matters. It's just as important as that half-hour together before the game but this time it's result orientated – depending on whether you have won or lost it takes on a different shape. It's such a bonding experience.

Hitting the town afterwards was all we had in rugby. It was an amateur game, we were never out of pocket but you couldn't make a living out of playing, not even through playing for Wales. It would help with getting employment, the fact that people knew who you were and you had a chance to sell your wares but it wouldn't do your job for you, it just gave you an opportunity. We just had the camaraderie and the fun, the enjoyment afterwards – you felt that it was well earned.

There was no social media back then, which was a very good thing considering all the characters we had in the squad! These days everyone has a camera on their phone and they are all looking to make a little name for themselves. People see the players as fair game now. Fortunately we could let off steam behind closed doors in that hour in the players' room. We'd play our little drinking games and say what we thought of each other. Whatever it was, you would get it out of your system and then we would be ready to go back out in public.

I wasn't a big drinker but I got drunk that night – and that's why I got drunk, because I wasn't a big drinker! I used to join in a round but once I knew that I'd had my fill, I would look for a flowerpot somewhere, with a wilting flower, so I could dispose of my beer.

After leaving the stadium we later found ourselves outside Jacksons, and Ringo, who was always a big character, had seen a few of his St Albans mates in the queue outside so he decided to join them to make sure they got in. When they reached the front, he looked at the doorman and said, "Mark Ring. There's four of us."

The doorman said, "Hang on, I'll go and see." He closed the door and came back about ten minutes later and said, "He's not in here, mate." And he slammed the door shut.

*

We travelled up to Scotland for our next game, full of confidence after beating England, but our bubble was to be burst as Scotland beat us 21–15. The game reminded me of something Meredydd James used to say, it was a bit like after the Lord Mayor's show. I had experienced a similar let-down shortly after Bridgend had beaten Australia and we had faced Pontypridd, who were a shadow of the great team they were to become in the Nineties, and promptly lost. You raise yourself to such a peak, it's near impossible to do it again in a short space of time.

*

I was dropped to the bench for the final game, against Ireland, but I never learnt why. I didn't see much of the ball against Scotland so didn't really have a chance to shine. I only found out I had been dropped when I went to the Cavalier in Ely in the week to see the boys. One of them said, "Hey Webby, you're out then."

I said, "Yes, I've been out since about one o'clock this afternoon."

He said, "No. You are out of the team to play Ireland." That's how it was in those days, you would read the team in the paper.

As it turned out, Ireland beat Wales that day – that's all I'm saying.

CHAPTER 7

The Rugby World Cup

To BEGIN WITH I found the 1987 Rugby World Cup – co-hosted by New Zealand and Australia – a great experience but it turned out to be one that was to leave me, quite literally, feeling as though I had been hit by a truck.

Just to be named in the squad was unbelievable, as I never expected to go. I never expected anything on the international front and was grateful for everything that came my way as it had been so difficult to break through in the first place. I always counted my blessings.

I had another reason to doubt my place on the plane, besides my natural pessimism – I was carrying an injury. Like a lot of my Cardiff mates, I used to play a bit of baseball in the summer and had twisted my knee so I was out for a while. As a result, I missed a few of the training sessions and so attended the final get-together before the squad was announced with some trepidation.

We had to endure a 600m striding session, so my heart was in my mouth as I knew that, if my fitness was in doubt, I would be found out. They practically told me that places were still up for grabs and if I didn't train then I would not be on the plane. As it happened, I broke the record.

They didn't announce the squad that evening and I was kept hanging on. As usual it wasn't until the following day, when they printed the Rugby World Cup squad in the newspaper, that I knew I had been selected. It was such a relief.

Realising that I could be away for anything up to six weeks, I had to ask my employers for time off. I had only just started a new job selling uPVC windows, but I had forewarned them that I might be picked for the Rugby World Cup. My request was granted – you could say that they saw it was a great window of opportunity for me! The only downside was I didn't get paid for the time I was away. Most of the boys lost money playing for Wales, even though the WRU paid us expenses, a daily allowance.

There was a real buzz amongst the players and supporters alike – it was the first ever Rugby World Cup and quite naturally everyone was excited. The concept of a global showpiece had been talked about for a number of years and so the anticipation was huge. The beauty of the tournament was the fact that the 16 top rugby playing nations were all gathered in one place at the same time, the best players in the world all on show, it was something that had never happened before. It was the first tournament of its kind and it saw rugby finally being placed on a world stage.

There was no lavish opening ceremony like you have today but there was an official players' reception in this large hall somewhere in Auckland. You had all these players, the best on the planet, just milling around. It was literally a who's who of world rugby. As I looked around, trying to take it all in, I spotted the All Black wing, John Kirwan. We all knew who the New Zealand boys were and, if anything, we were a bit in awe of them. At the time Kirwan was perhaps the best wing in world rugby. He was a big lad who, with blond hair and a GI haircut, reminded me of that Russian goliath, Ivan Drago, who gave Rocky the toughest fight of his life in *Rocky IV*. As I was looking, he caught my gaze and said, "It's Webbe, isn't it?"

I was chuffed by the fact that he knew who I was. That acknowledgement made me think, 'Hang on, why shouldn't he know me?' That's when the penny dropped and I told myself, 'I'm an international player.' It was only a small moment but it changed me. I grew a little bit in my own eyes.

I was about to go over and have a chat with him when the lights were dimmed and the hall was filled with pumping music, interspersed with the purr of a highly tuned engine. Then some huge curtains opened and this shining new Mazda sports car – it was just gleaming – crept in with its engine growling and drove up onto a podium that began rotating slowly.

It turned out to be the prize for the scorer of what was judged to be the tournament's best try. It was an amazing car. Ringo nudged me and said, "We have got to win that car!" That led to us spending hours trying to come up with all these moves just to be in with a shout of winning that Mazda.

They weren't that realistic but eventually we settled on this one move where the inside centre went from inside out, the outside centre came from outside in, the outside-half looped around and popped the ball off to me coming from deep off the wing and through the middle, where both centres would have taken away their opponents, giving me a free run down the field and under the posts. Naturally we called the move Mazda. It never worked in training – it was just ridiculous – and it never worked in a game either.

*

We had been drawn in Pool 2 alongside Ireland, Canada and those peace-loving South Sea Islanders, Tonga! We were based in New Zealand for the pool stages and while I liked the country, everything closed by 10pm! A lot of the places had small populations and so you had to make your own entertainment. Fortunately that was never a problem when Ringo and I were around.

One of things we came up with was wrestling matches. It wasn't full-on wrestling; you would just try to lift each other off the floor. I was pretty good at wrestling, the only boys I used to struggle against were Rowland Phillips – he was like a crocodile, with a long body and stumpy legs, so you couldn't get underneath him – and Stuart Evans who was so big he was just stuck to the floor.

Then Ringo and I decided to organise a pool tournament. We all entered and put money in and it was a straight knockout between 32 of us. As it turned out, Ringo and I made it to the final and played each other – everyone thought that it had been rigged – it wasn't. When we realised we were both in the final we decided to split the pot no matter who won, so, of course, everyone thought it was contrived but it couldn't have been. We had beaten everyone we came up against.

With all that money in our pockets there was only one thing to do midweek in New Zealand – go to the pub. This was early on, when we were still acclimatising and the games hadn't started, so we weren't too worried about drinking. We found a pub not far from our hotel and, when we walked in, half the Scottish team were there, along with some of the Irish boys, and they were already in full flow. We pulled up a couple of chairs and set about teaching our Celtic cousins some drinking games. We had great fun.

John Jeffrey, the Great White Shark as he was known – not least due to his white-blond hair and lack of any suntan whatsoever, thought he was also one hell of a flanker who hunted outside-halves down and gobbled them up – was one of the ringleaders and so became an instant target. One of the games, called Itchy Coo, saw us all sat around the table with pints in front of us. The object of the game was to do exactly what the person sat to your right had previously done.

I started it off and said, "Itchy coo, coo, coo, coo," and I rubbed my hands across my face and had a little drink and it went on to the next person, who copied me, and it went all the way around until it came back to me. The second time I said, "Itchy coo, coo, coo, coo," and turned to the person sat to my left and rubbed his face three times with the tips of my fingers.

Now this was in the days when people could actually smoke in pubs so there were overflowing ashtrays on the tables and when it came to Ringo, who had strategically placed himself next to John Jeffrey, his fingers had been dipped in cigarette ash, and his hands went all over the Great White Shark's face. As the game continued his face became even more covered. Everyone was in stiches apart from John Jeffrey, who had no idea what was going on – not even when they started calling him the Great Grey Shark. It was halfway through the evening by the time he'd seen his face in a mirror and shouted, "Bloody Webby!"

We were staying in the same hotel as Scotland and I will never forget seeing him come down for breakfast the following morning with his face still half covered in cigarette ash.

*

It was great being there with all the players, bumping into them when you were out, drinking together, talking and getting to know them. It was just like a massive rugby tour. You may question international players drinking during the biggest tournament of their lives but, when you were all in the pub or club together, you were the majority, there was such a gang of players, all together, doing the same thing. There was no one who was an alcoholic and couldn't wait to get on it but, also, there wasn't anyone who would say, "No thanks, there's training in the morning." Everyone seemed to have self-control and knew when enough was enough, time for bed.

The only real exceptions were the All Blacks. When I was on tour in New Zealand and at the World Cup, I rarely saw an All Black out and about with a drink in his hands. With their lifestyle, I think they were geared for professionalism long before the game went professional. Even then, they were professional in their outlook, their approach and their attitude. They were never outwardly loutish; they were always respectable. You can see why they are the best at what they do. With the respect and the love they have for the game, they are professional in every single way.

Every New Zealand child has the ambition to pull on that famous black jersey. I'm sure that there's going to be one kid who thinks, 'I want to be the first player to actually give his life wearing the New Zealand rugby jersey.' They basically would run through walls for that jersey, they would do anything. 'I want to die on the field.' That's ambition for you!

*

I was on the bench for our opening game – a 13–6 win against the Irish in Wellington – with Ieuan Evans getting the nod but I was given the number 14 jersey for the next game against Tonga in Palmerston North. Fortunately, our friend Bloomfield wasn't in the Tonga side that day but, as it turned out, they didn't need him as there was a far more lethal player in their ranks, as I will shortly explain. Although I didn't see him, Bloomfield was in New Zealand as a spectator, as Stuart Evans recalls running into him in a pub one night. Now it takes a lot to spook big Stuart but his heart began beating faster when Bloomfield spotted him and walked over – 'here we go again' he thought – but fortunately he just pulled up a chair and had a few pints.

The game started off brilliantly for me and I came off my right wing and took the ball off Kevin Hopkins and dummied to Hadley, sending the full-back the wrong way, and scored in the corner. Later in the same half Paul Moriarty burst into their 22, the ball came back and Ringo put a chip in, which I managed to gather, and I squeezed in at the corner. It was a perfect start to my Rugby World Cup but my luck was about to change.

In the second half we had a scrum on the halfway line, with a big blindside, so Jonathan Davies, who had come on for Malcolm Dacey, went right and fed Paul Thorburn, who had come up from full-back, and he put me away. Unfortunately, Ete'aki, their full-back, came from nowhere. If you want to know what he looks like, look at my chin as his face is still imprinted on it! He just took off like a human Exocet missile and his head slammed into this little switch that everyone has on the bottom of their chin – if you tap it hard enough it's 'Lights out and good night!'

His head came in and I collapsed as though I had been shot. I only know all this from watching the video back several days later. I just hit the deck and was out cold. I heard that Ete'aki actually lost an arm in a fight with a guy who had a machete a few years later – that's the honest truth – but I suppose that it didn't stop him playing as he didn't need arms to tackle!

Now, as I have said, you only had two reserves back then – they weren't substitutes because you couldn't make any unforced changes. Malcolm Dacey had already gone off injured, to be replaced by Jonathan Davies, and Stuart Evans had been stretchered off with a broken ankle (Steve Blackmore had come on), so there was no one to replace me. I was injured and should have gone off but we would have been down to 14 men, so I stayed on.

I found out later that Clive Rowlands had told Ringo, "Just try to keep him out of trouble. Don't give the ball to him." When I finally saw the game back on television, Tonga put up this huge bomb and everyone was looking at each other saying, "You take it!" It bounced a couple of times and eventually Ringo got the ball, with three or four Tongans bearing down on him, so he threw the ball out to me! I was near our 22 and I just set off, swerved a couple of times, inside and outside, and scored under the posts for what was a pretty good try... even if I didn't remember a second of it. Ringo claims that he had to shout at me to put the ball down once I had crossed the line but there's no way he would have kept up with me!

I had scored a hat-trick in the Rugby World Cup and couldn't remember a thing! I was still out of it in the changing rooms after the game. I'm told I turned to Ringo and asked, "Who are all these people?" I didn't even recognise my own teammates. If they had had head injury assessments back then, they would still be doing the tests today!

On a daily basis, the best tries were featured and put forward into the final of the Mazda competition and that try was one of the runners up – John Kirwan won it with a fantastic try in the opening game against Italy. It was a phenomenal try to be fair, but he wasn't concussed at the time!

The most gutting thing – even now, some 32 years later – was that after the game Clive Rowlands took me aside and said, "Glenn, I'm afraid we're going to have to send you home mate." I felt my whole world come to an end.

I said, "What do you mean?"

"You're going to have to go home," he repeated. "There's nothing we can do about it, you're concussed. We are only looking after your own best interests."

I begged him not to but when I realised that there was nothing that I could do to change his mind I started to get a little angry. I felt as though I had been used.

"You're not looking after my interests at all," I said. "You're looking after your own!"

"Oh, don't say that Glenn."

"Look," I said. "If you were looking after my interests you would have taken me off the field at the time, when I was injured. You only kept me out there because we would have been down to 14 men and Tonga would have beaten us. That's the only reason you left me out there, you didn't care about me then."

He wasn't having any of it and that was the end of my World Cup.

I know player welfare and concussion is big news today but this wasn't today, it was back then, and I still feel angry and aggrieved about it. I'd travelled halfway around the world only to be sent home. My anger was all down to the fact that I had found it so difficult to get selected in the first place, it would have been a golden opportunity to state my case – the world was watching and there were so many games.

Stuart Evans had to go home as well because he had a broken ankle and I had to carry his bags! To make matters worse, as

I was pushing him through the airport in a wheelchair, some supporters started asking him for his autograph and didn't recognise me at all. They thought I was a porter! To be honest, if I had to go all that way home with anyone, I'm glad that it was with Stuart as we had a bit of a chuckle on the way back. But just to add insult to injury, as we crossed over the Equator, somewhere out there, Mark Titley was on an aeroplane heading the other way to take my place in the squad!

*

As for results, Wales hammered Canada 40–9 in the final group game to set up a quarter-final against the English. Wales won 16–3 – John Devereux had a fantastic game and was easily man of the match, he scored a try and his hand-offs were fantastic. I watched the games on my own at home. It was hard to watch, to be honest. It was a strange feeling of being part of it and not at the same time. There you were, watching from the other side of the world, whereas a week earlier you had been there taking part. I suppose that I should let it go but it's very difficult to do so.

You may think that it was different watching the semi-final as New Zealand absolutely thrashed Wales, 49–6, in Brisbane, but I always wanted my friends, teammates and my country to do well whether I played or not.

Somehow the boys bounced back and went on to have the best finish in any Rugby World Cup by claiming third place after beating Australia in Rotorua. Hadley squeezed in at the corner in the dying seconds and Thorburn converted from the touchline to win a classic, 22–21.

At least the year ended on a high as I was recalled to the side for a game against the USA in Cardiff in November. It turned out to be a walkover and I picked up a try, finishing off a planned move as we won 46–0.

CHAPTER 8

Touring New Zealand

THE 1988 WALES tour to New Zealand was a bit of a historic occasion for all the wrong reasons – we were completely blown out of the water. People were queuing up to question the wisdom of such a tour following on from the record 49–6 hammering in the World Cup semi-final less than a year before, but in fairness to the WRU these things are planned well in advance. I don't think that the WRU realised just where we were at that time. No one outside of New Zealand could have foreseen the World Cup humiliation and it was too late to turn around and say we didn't want to go.

Perhaps the WRU thought we might have given them a game as we had only played New Zealand 12 times in 82 years at that point, and had actually won three times, so our losing streak only stretched back 35 years instead of the 66 years it stands at today.

While I don't think there were too many players happy to go on that tour, to me it was another trip away and I couldn't wait to go – but it was tough. The training was tough, the games were tough and the Tests were tough.

There were no easy games at all. The New Zealand coach, Alex Wyllie, said that had it been his team touring he wouldn't have accepted the itinerary! Even the provincial players were as big, as physical and as fit as us, and, most of the time, they were better at playing rugby. We played six provincial games, only winning against Hawke's Bay and Otago, and reached new depths of despair through conceding over 50 points in each of the two Tests and only scoring one try in reply.

*

Whenever I travelled away with Wales, we would usually have to share a room and my roommate would always be my old Cardiff & District Youth teammate, Mark Ring. No matter who we were paired with I would say, "Come on, out you go. I'm rooming with Ringo."

We always tried to get one up on each other in a joking kind of way. On one occasion we were travelling together by car to a Welsh training session down in west Wales – they used to hold them in different places to engage with the public – and I had a packet of Maltesers. I asked him if he wanted one and he said no but I knew that he wanted one really, so I kept on offering. He was really stubborn and kept on turning the offer down. When I came down to the last three in the packet I said, "Here you are, you can finish them off," and put them down.

"I told you," he said, "I don't want any."

We stopped to get some petrol soon after and I left him in the car on his own. When I got back, I noticed that the packet had been moved – I knew full well that there were only three left but that he didn't know that I knew that – and I started giggling to myself and picked it up to find that there was one missing.

"I knew it!" I said. "Why didn't you just admit it? You should have said, 'Yes Glenn, I would like a Malteser, thank you for asking.'" I went on for a few minutes but he just remained quiet.

When we arrived, not long after, he reached in the side pocket of the car and withdrew a Malteser and handed it to me saying, "There you are, I told you I didn't want one." It was typical of the games we played.

On the New Zealand tour I had brought along this reusable

banger. It was a small metal hinge, with a spring, that you placed a cap in and set before placing it underneath an object, such as a mug, and when you lifted the object up, it would snap shut and make a bang. I used to leave it all over the place. Ringo would pick up his shoe and it would go bang! He would pick up his kit bag and bang!

He had this habit of turning his pillow over, once he was in bed, before going to sleep, so one night I put the banger under his pillow. When he lifted the pillow up, it went bang! "Webbe! What did you do that for?! I'm awake now!"

On that tour Ringo had this new bottle of aftershave made by Paco Rabanne. It had just come out and smelt lovely. So while he was in the shower I decided to use it. When he came out his nose twitched and he asked, "Have you been using my Paco Rabanne?"

"No," I said. "I have my own aftershave."

"Well it smells like it."

The next time I went to use it I noticed that there was a little mark on the bottle. That didn't stop me, I just rubbed the mark off, used the aftershave, and added a new mark.

When he came back in the room, he sniffed the air and said, "You've been using my Paco Rabanne!"

"I haven't," I protested.

"Well I marked the bottle," he replied smugly and went over to pick it up. A look of confusion crept across his face as he studied the bottle. He knew I had used it but he couldn't prove it!

Soon afterwards we had a training session and I decided to take my banger along – I'd have all sorts of fun at lunchtime leaving it under people's plates – but I couldn't find it.

"Come on," said Ringo. "We're going to be late."

"I can't find my banger," I said. "Have you seen it?"

"I haven't seen your childish toy," he replied. "Are you coming or what?"

"I'll follow you down," I said and spent the next five minutes looking for it without any joy. I was even late for training and had a telling-off. I know it was only a little thing but it upset me and I was in a bad mood for the rest of the day.

That evening we were getting ready to go out and while Ringo was in the shower, I picked up his aftershave and BANG! I jumped out of my skin. He had beaten me at my own game!

We had so much fun winding people up. It may appear childish but when you are away from home and in what can sometimes be a pressurised situation, it's a vital release of tension. We weren't the first to behave like schoolboys and we certainly haven't been the last – I'm just glad we never stumbled across a golf buggy on our adventures!

*

Touring New Zealand was one hell of an experience, not least as the game was still amateur and the All Blacks were so far ahead of the rest of the world. Just to speak to their players, after you had plucked up enough courage to introduce yourself that is, was something to treasure. They had a completely different mindset – with them it was never a case of 'are we going to win?' It was always, 'How much are we going to win by?'

They were talking about things like taking bone marrow extracts from kids aged eight or nine to predict their growth capacity. They could say things like, this kid is going to end up being 6ft 5ins but they have him playing in the centre, so they could change his position. Or it may be the other way around, he may only reach 5ft 10ins and they have him in the second row. What they were doing was trying to match their playing positions with their growth potential. It was just so scientific... like something you would expect to find in the old East Germany.

We also learned that in school they would play barefoot up to a certain age, not because of stamping but to discourage kicking – because it would hurt – and so encourage handling skills. There were lots of things going on along those lines.

Even the watching public were streets ahead of us back home, as I was to find out. Just as during the Five Nations, I wouldn't always wear the WRU gear and would dress down to go under the radar when I went out, preferring to just be myself and not give anything away. On one such occasion this woman looked at me and said, "Aren't you Glenn Webbe? Who plays for Wales?"

"Yeah, I am," I said. I was quite chuffed that she had recognised me.

"I've admired you," she said. "I've seen you play on television. You're very fast and I do like your play."

"Oh, thank you very much," I said.

"But there's one thing I've noticed." She hadn't finished. "You stand too shallow, you don't stand deep enough when you are expecting the ball."

I felt quite offended but she was actually right. I had been told the same thing time and again by coaches. That summed up the rugby knowledge of the New Zealand public. This woman, who could have been anyone, recognised me out of a sea of faces and she knew the game so well that she identified a little fault in my game.

*

I played in the 15–13 win against Otago and was picked for the first Test in Christchurch. I had missed the chance to play against New Zealand in the World Cup after being sent home with concussion so this was the first time that I had faced the haka. It was certainly an experience. Everyone, from all over the world, has heard of the haka. It's something that they need to do – it's all part and parcel of the All Blacks' brand but I think it definitely gives them an unfair advantage. It allows them to let off steam and vent their anger, if you like. The worst part is that it's a challenge that you are not allowed to respond to. You are not allowed to turn away, you are not allowed to ridicule it, you just have to stand there and take what you are given. It's like someone being allowed to insult you, call you the worst possible names going, and you can't do anything about it.

Saying that, it didn't intimidate me any more than hearing a team shouting one to ten in the next changing room. I just tried to take it all in – just watching who pulled the funniest face. I wondered what it all meant to each individual, because it is obviously a tribal thing and a lot of the New Zealanders aren't tribal, they are ex-pats, so does it mean as much to them? But no matter what I thought, every single one of them gave it 100 per cent. They really dug in deep and gave it everything they possible could.

Then they kicked off and hammered us 52–3! We need a haka, that's the reason why we lost!

The New Zealand side that day was packed with All Black legends, but when you look at our line-up there were plenty of players who are remembered today as being stars – yet it was like men playing against boys.

New Zealand
15 John Gallagher, 14 John Kirwan, 13 Joe Stanley,
12 Warwick Taylor, 11 Terry Wright, 10 Grant Fox,
9 Bruce Deans.
1 Steve McDowall, 2 Sean Fitzpatrick, 3 Richard Loe,
4 Murray Pierce, 5 Gary Whetton, 6 Alan Whetton,
7 Michael Jones, 8 Buck Shelford (c)

Wales
15 Tony Clement, 14 Ieuan Evans, 13 John Devereux,
12 Mark Ring, 11 Glenn Webbe, 10 Jonathan Davies,
9 Robert Jones.
1 Staff Jones, 2 Kevin Phillips, 3 Dai Young,
4 Bob Norster (c), 5 Phil May, 6 Rowland Phillips,
7 David Bryant, 8 Paul Moriarty.

This was one game where I didn't mind being on the left

Glenn's first day at Herbert Thompson Primary School

With his classmates

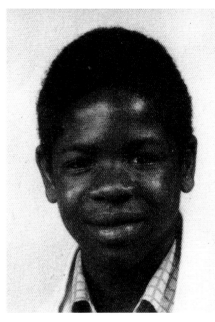

Cheeky chap at primary school

Eleven-year-old Glenn starting Glan Ely High School

Let's play ball: Glenn captaining his school baseball team

Nineteen-year-old Glenn

Jubilation! In the changing rooms after Bridgend beat Australia in October 1981

Taking his place as part of a Whitbread Merit Table Select XV in 1983, not long after stepping up to senior rugby

Bridgend team photo 1990–91

Shrugging off an attempted tackle

(© Huw Evans Agency)

Glenn playing in
a match against
Newbridge
(© Huw Evans Agency)

Contact: in the
blue and white
of Bridgend

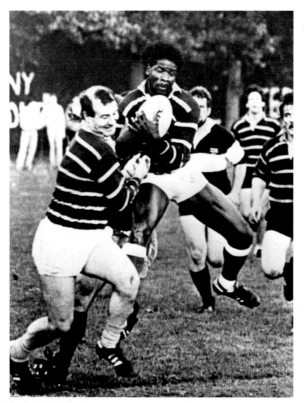

My ball!

In action at a
packed Brewery Field

On trial: wearing the white of the Possibles against the Probables in red during a Welsh trial

If the cap fits: Glenn modelling his senior cap

Glenn reflects on wearing the red jersey

The big time: making a break against England in Cardiff in 1987

Wales's Rugby World Cup
squad, 1987

1987 World Cup teammates,
L–R: Jonathan Davies, John
Devereux, Glenn and Mark Ring

History makers. L–R: Dai Bryant,
John Devereux, Mike Griffiths,
Glenn and Richard Diplock in
training before Wales versus
Romania in 1988

Birthday boy: Glenn surprises fellow wing Richard Diplock with a cake on his birthday while at Heathrow's departure lounge

Boys on tour: Bridgend's trip to Atlanta, 1990

A different Bridgend kit this time – dressed up as Santas!

Bridgend former players' reunion in 2017

Best friends: socialising with Mark Ring and Mike Budd

Roommates: on tour in Bermuda with Ringo

With Robbie James

With Ringpiece

Check it out: one of
Glenn's coolest soul-
glo styles

Sister Act. L–R: Jelly, Humie, Bernadette, Chunky Bam Bam, Celena, Spooney and Vrick

Glenn and his sisters gather to celebrate their father's 80th birthday

Date night: Glenn and Sally

Greatest match: Glenn and
Sally on their wedding day
in Bermuda

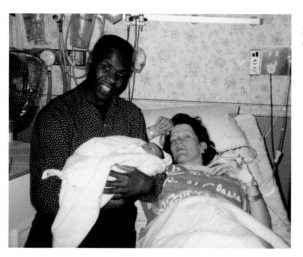

First kiss: Mr and Mrs Webbe

Proud dad: with daughter Lily

Safe pair of hands: Sally and daughter number two, Marcy

Mr Zeng: Glenn gives his
biographer, Geraint Thomas,
a lesson in arm wrestling

Boss man: at his kitchen
showrooms
(© Steve Phillips)

wing – it was New Zealand after all, and it brought me up against John Kirwan. However, he scored four tries down my wing. The closest I came to laying hands on him came after the final whistle when we swapped jerseys. There was nothing I could do about it. Every time they came, there was an obvious overlap. If I stayed out, players inside would go through, and if I came in, they would feed them outside; there were always numbers there. I hardly touched the ball. It was just a ridiculous state of affairs. The joke going around at the time was, 'What time are Wales kicking off against New Zealand?' 'Every two minutes!' It was an onslaught.

There's a point in every game when you know whether you have won or lost – on that occasion we got there within 15 minutes! We knew that the game was over as a competition. We were just paying it lip service. They were running it for fun. If they didn't score, it was only because they were getting in each other's way.

My rugby career flashed before my eyes and I was playing for my school or Canton Youth, getting hammered all over again. The only problem was, I couldn't do my old trick and stand in front of the posts and run any penalty kicks that fell short back at them as, being the All Blacks, their 10, Grant Fox, nailed them all!

It was the worst hiding I had been on the wrong end of at any level – I had never had more than half a century scored against me before. Not even on a park pitch. It was so demoralising. You couldn't look up. No one wanted to look you in the eye. You couldn't say anything, there was nothing you could physically do, it was humiliating. It was just tackle, tackle, tackle and then tackle again. A lot of players went missing in action. A few said they were injured but they weren't necessarily – I don't want to name names but players who we thought were our go-to men went missing.

I think even our coaches, Tony Gray and Derek Quinnell, conceded.

Lots of sides get hammered today points-wise, but we also

took a physical hammering which you never see today. The way rugby was played back then was completely different to how it's played today. The New Zealand pack was like a mob. They were just a gang of forwards running at you. Wherever the ball was, there was a gang of All Blacks, just like a big black cloud. The game was totally structureless compared to how it is now with phase after phase. It was just a gang of eight and then 'boom!', they would obliterate anything with the ball if it didn't have a black jersey on. It was just unbelievable.

If you look at the Eighties, the closest thing we had to the All Blacks' style of play in Welsh rugby was Neath. They were even known as the Welsh All Blacks – and it wasn't just because of the colour of their jerseys. They used to steamroller everyone, as well.

Being rucked by the New Zealand eight and coming out the other side, having lived to tell the tale, is my claim to fame – because it hurt. Remember, this was when you were allowed to ruck. They would just run over you and you were part of that ball. It was just the sheer numbers. They were so tight together – they would join up before they even got to the ruck. To get so tight, to have that many people covering such a small amount of space, and to run so low and hard, was the result of years and years of technical training. You don't see it now – but I still do sometimes when I close my eyes! I still think there's room in today's game for a decent ruck. It would clean everything out.

You would try to get the ball. You saw it so infrequently you would try to make the most of what little possession you had. So when you did get it, it was your opportunity to do something with it, but invariably Michael Jones, their world-class seven, would get a little finger to your boot and drag you in and, a few seconds later, there's eight of them and you're on the other side watching their scrum-half pick the ball up.

Being hammered like that just made me more determined – I was given a seven out of ten in the players' ratings after the game against Otago, while everyone else in my side had fours or fives. I was enjoying the fact that it was just a simple role to play – we weren't getting any ball and it was just a case of throwing yourself into tackles. I used to enjoy tackling. I probably did one too many and popped my shoulder.

*

We had two more provincial games before the second Test, Hawke's Bay, and North Auckland. I picked up an injury in the latter game. We were dropping like flies. Once again, even after I was injured, they kept me on the field because there wasn't anyone to bring on – I was left wondering what I had to do to be taken off injured in a Welsh jersey. I had to miss the next training session but was picked to play in the second Test but I missed the team run-out. I don't think that they believed I had a problem with my shoulder so they sent me to hospital for an X-ray, which showed that I had a hairline fracture – I have still got a lump on my shoulder. I don't know whether they were disappointed for me or just disappointed that they had lost another player. I was disappointed that they hadn't taken my word that I was injured – I would do anything to play for Wales. I know how difficult it is to get picked in the first place.

Even the captaincy was cursed, with Bleddyn Bowen, the initial tour captain, breaking his wrist in the second game, then Bob Norster, who became captain, was also injured and was replaced by Jonathan Davies. In all, we lost so many players to injury that five replacements had to be flown out.

*

Off the field we did our best to bond as a squad. The majority of players were from Llanelli – we used to make songs up about them, 'If I were a Scarlet. Urgh!' There was an east verses west thing going on. But there were no real cliques, it was a case of everyone mucking in. There were a number of Welsh speakers and, to some non-Welsh speakers, it seemed as soon as you walked in the room they would switch to Welsh so you wouldn't understand – but it wasn't like that at all. If a player always spoke Welsh to someone, then they were just doing what comes naturally. It wasn't a case of being a clique.

Despite the poor results, there was a good craic amongst the boys and at the heart of it all, as always, was Ringo. Neath's Jeremy Pugh had made the trip – we used to call him the Builth Wells Bully, although at less charitable times he was referred to as Piggy Pugh. Now while as far as Neath may have been concerned he was the wisecracking prop forward, he couldn't lace Ringo's boots and Ringo used to tie him up in absolute knots. Ringo was so direct; he could put you down like that. I was probably nicer.

There was one occasion, I think we were playing against Hawke's Bay, when a big fight broke out. There was this prop, who was only 19, as we found out afterwards, who gave Pugh a hammering. His nose was split across the bridge and his eyes had gone. On the long coach journey afterwards, Pugh was going on about how he had had the better of this prop but, in fact, Pugh had been doing the front crawl while this kid was just picking him off. He landed three right on his snout.

We stopped off in this pub called the Boar's Head. We gathered some tables around and sat in this big circle and had a few drinks. Now above where we were sitting a big boar's head was mounted on the wall, hence the name of the pub. When Pugh got up to go to the toilet I went up to Tudor Jones, our physio, and said, "Have you got some plasters?"

I then climbed up on a chair and stuck them across the boar's snout. We then shuffled the chairs around so that when Pugh came back, the only empty chair was directly below the boar's head. We all pretended to be talking and so he just sat down.

Then people started coming up to him saying, "Alright Jeremy? Can I get a picture?" And he sat there smiling, with a big plaster across his nose, sitting below a boar's head with a plaster across its nose! People took photograph after photograph and he didn't have a clue.

*

The second Test, in Auckland, was just as one-sided as the first, although Jonathan Davies scored a fantastic individual try having run the length of the field. Jonathan was very vocal about the state of Welsh rugby after that tour. In fairness, he was just head and shoulders above the rest of the Welsh team so you could understand his frustration. I loved his attitude – he was a pure winner and he was so able. It was as if he had too much pace for an outside-half to be honest and a lot of the time he used to just run. He would have made a great wing – a left wing!

Although some labelled him outspoken, he was just making people aware of the gulf that existed between New Zealand and Wales. The WRU took immediate action and blamed the coach. Out went the affable Tony Gray and in came John Ryan, who was quite the disciplinarian.

CHAPTER 9

Watching Wales from the bench

THE 1988 FIVE Nations was the most successful for Wales since the Golden Generation of Gareth, Gerald, Merv, JPR and the other household names. Captained by Bleddyn Bowen we picked up a Triple Crown and narrowly missed out on a Grand Slam by a couple of points, but I spent the whole campaign – apart from the last few minutes – sat on the bench.

It was just great to be part of the squad. I was gutted that I didn't quite make it across the line and get selected to start in any of the games, but back then it was just a small squad of 19 players who were actually involved on match day, so I was just happy to be part of it all.

Our first game was away to England and the boys played some fantastic rugby, with Adrian Hadley scoring two tries to help us to an 11–3 win. Although I didn't make it onto the field, I was at the centre of the action during the after-match dinner and formalities, so to speak. As with any away trip, I had stocked up on some props – not the scrummaging kind – and was ready for a bit of post-match entertainment. One of my accessories was a fake hand, which I had liberated from a dummy in a shop window. I tucked it up the sleeve of my blazer and when I shook hands with people it came off in their hands! It caused quite a bit of confusion, followed by laughter.

I also packed a laughter box – it was one of those small contraptions that, when you pressed a button, gave out a recording of laughter which, admittedly, got a bit annoying after the ninth or tenth time. Now, I had no way of knowing how useful it would be as the English captain, Mike Harrison, proved to be as funny as a high tackle during his speech. As we all sat there witnessing tumbleweed roll past his jokes, I decided to help him out and reached for the laughing box.

Apparently, such behaviour wasn't the done thing at HQ and Mick Skinner, the English blindside flanker, took exception and stormed over, grabbed the laughter box and dumped it in my pint. I responded like any self-respecting Ely boy and said, "Let's sort this out in the car park." There's no doubt we would have scrapped but we were intercepted by a posse of teammates and committee as we were walking out. They tried to reason with us and in the end the English team manager, Roger Uttley, suggested we have an arm wrestle in order to sort out our differences.

Skinner agreed and no doubt licked his lips thinking he would annihilate a wing, but he was in for a shock as I beat him three times in a row. I have always been pretty strong and used to do a lot of sit-ups, press-ups and pull-ups – even now I still manage to do 1,000 press-ups in 25 minutes – and I used to win a bit of money arm wrestling. It was nothing serious but you tend to get a bit of a reputation, so whenever I was out around the pubs people would come up and challenge me, and most of the time I would win.

In fairness, he took it fairly well and, as is always the way, we had a few pints together afterwards, although his pride was definitely hurt.

Shortly after returning home I was summoned to the WRU headquarters. I was shown the official team photograph and asked to explain myself – there I was, stood, with my arms folded, with one black hand and one white hand! That's the honest truth – I can't believe that no one spotted me but the official Wales Triple Crown team photograph was published

103

along with my fake hand. I was reprimanded by WRU secretary Ray Williams, but it was worth it!

*

Next up was a home game against Scotland and once again the boys turned on the magic – Ieuan Evans finished off a great move in which Ringo showed an amazing pair of hands to pick a ball up off his toes and put him into space, before Ieuan sidestepped a couple of times to touch down under the posts. Then Jonathan Davies scored a brilliant individual try, following up on his own grubber kick through a flat-footed Scottish defence, after being fed the ball by Robert Jones with a reverse pass from a five-metre scrum. The final score was 25–20.

It was on to Lansdowne Road next to play Ireland with a first Triple Crown for eight years at stake. Paul Moriarty picked up from a scrum five metres out to seal a 12–9 win, setting up a shot at the Grand Slam – something Wales hadn't achieved since 1978.

As great as the Arms Park was, we could have done with a roof as it rained non-stop – it wasn't a very nice day at all. Ieuan Evans and Adrian Hadley were on the wings. It was a vintage French backline with Serge Blanco at full-back, Jean-Baptiste Lafond and Patrice Lagisquet on the wings and Marc Andrieu and Philippe Sella in the centre, Jean-Patrick Lescarboura and Pierre Berbizier at half-back.

France led 10–3 when Bleddyn Bowen started a move off and passed to Jonathan Davies, who drew his man and passed to Ringo, who fed Ieuan Evans on the wing. Evans kicked ahead and he and Ringo both dived to touch the ball down. Now I'm sure that Ringo got there first but Evans was awarded the try and was injured in the process. I replaced him with about five minutes to go, with the game still in the balance. I still had time for a couple of runs but the French managed to hold on to win 10–9.

Wales would have to wait another 17 years, until 2005, for a Grand Slam under Mike Ruddock. It's difficult to explain why Wales had such a poor record during the late Eighties and Nineties. The game had definitely undergone a transition, with teams being coached like never before with planned moves and tactics worked out down to the finest detail beforehand. Wales had basically been left behind. We still tried to play a game that relied upon individual flair but I suppose we didn't have enough flair players to carry this off. We basically relied upon Jonathan Davies to tell us what to do!

We have more than caught up now and I think there is still more to come.

*

Unless it's of your own choosing, you never know that your last international is your last. As it turned out my final cap came in December 1988 at home to Romania and it was a game that was to go down in history because we lost to the eastern Europeans for the first and only time!

It had promised to be such a special occasion as there were six Bridgend players selected to play for Wales that day: four in the backline – myself and Richard Diplock on the wings, John Devereux and Mike Hall in the centres – and David Bryant and Mike Griffiths up front. I even think our hooker, Wayne Hall, was in the squad somewhere, so, as you can imagine, there was a tremendous air of excitement and pride down the Brewery Field.

Dai Bryant, at openside flanker, was a very good player who had been one of the few boys to enhance his reputation on the New Zealand tour, never having taken a backward step. He required 21 stitches in a head wound and acquired some scars on his back, from the rucking, which took around nine months to heal properly. Mike Griffiths was a tough prop forward who went on to tour Australia with the British & Irish Lions the following season. He also went on to join Cardiff, but good luck to him. Most of all I was really pleased for Dippy, as we called him, to get a cap on the wing. He was a very good player: he was pacey, ran straight and hard, and he knew where the try-line was.

John Devereux, another to make the Lions tour the following season, was a really solid centre, well-defined and very muscular – he looks the same today to be honest with you! He had such flexibility for a big bloke. I used to watch him stretching in the warm-up and not only could he easily touch his toes, he could put his palms on the floor. He could fold himself in half like a penknife. He also had a 'handgun' (handoff) which was better than most people could punch!

As for Mike Hall, he was actually chosen ahead of Mark Ring as he was a firm favourite of the new Wales coach, John Ryan, and there was a feeling that he wanted him to play no matter what. At the time Mike was a student at Cambridge University and there was a tradition with Wales which said you weren't allowed to play for your club the week before your first cap. The Romania game was on the Saturday and Cambridge were playing their Varsity game against Oxford at Twickenham on the Tuesday before. The Varsity game is the reason most top players end up going to the big two universities in the first place – perhaps I should have gone but I don't think they offered degrees in rugby songs or practical jokes!

I remember Mike being told by the Welsh coaches during training that if he was selected then he wouldn't be able to play in the Varsity game – they made it clear that it was the Varsity game or Wales. Mike Hall responded with, "Well, I'll play in the Varsity game." No one expected that, least of all John Ryan.

As for myself – I should never have played. Ryan had told me that I was selected to play but I told him I wasn't fit because I was still recovering from a hamstring tear. I had made that clear the week before when the squad first assembled. I even asked, "Why have you named me?"

Ryan just said, "Well, we'll see how it goes," and he still named me in the team.

I had quite a lot of hamstring problems during my career. I suppose it came from trying to come back too early – pressure being put on you and you being keen to get back. If you imagine an injured hamstring as being like a lacerated elastic band, where it's down to its last thread but it feels OK and is still taut – then when it goes, it's gone. I've probably still got scars upon scars on my hamstrings, it was a big problem.

The Varsity game came and went and the Welsh team was announced publicly on the Wednesday. When I turned up for training, Mike Hall was in the changing room. When I asked him what he was doing there, he said that Ryan had asked him to train. We went out on the field and Ryan said to me, "You're injured, aren't you Glenn? So you're not going to be able to make it on Saturday." That's when the penny dropped. He thought I wouldn't play because I wasn't fit and if he brought Mike Hall along, he could take my place at the last minute having played in the Varsity game.

So, I said, "Actually, I'm OK."

He said, "What?"

I replied, "I'm fit to play."

He barked back, "You will have to have a fitness test."

"That's alright," I said. I strapped my leg up better than Tutankhamun – it was really killing me but I knew exactly what they were doing. They wanted to use me as a scapegoat but I was going to put a stop to their little game.

Ryan tried to kill me during the training session and at the end he said to me, "Right, you're going to do some extra work now." And he had me sprinting the ladders up and down the field, dropping to the floor on the try-line every time, but I did it all.

Afterwards he asked how I was feeling and I said, "Fine."

So then he said, "Where's Ring tonight?" Ringo had missed the session.

"I don't know," I replied. Actually he was talking to David Bishop who had already gone north.

"I've heard he's talking to League scouts. You know, tell

me." I didn't say a word and he walked off. The next thing I knew, on the Thursday, there was a late change to the team, with Mike Hall coming into the centre for Mark Ring who had been dropped.

*

As the history books will tell you, we lost 9–15 that day. Romania played well and deserved to win. It was just awful to lose any game but it really felt like Wales just didn't turn up on the day. It was one of those games in which you always think that you are going to win, no matter what, and before you know it, the final whistle is there. I know that I didn't contribute a great deal because I wasn't on for that long. It was a strange feeling for me as I knew that I wasn't fit to play. I only lasted 20 minutes of the game before my hamstring went. Paul Thorburn, who was on the bench, had to come on and play on the wing.

You may question why I took to the field knowing that I wasn't fully fit, but at the time I was resentful of the fact that Ryan and his selectors seemed to have tried to manipulate me in order to pick Mike Hall – who had chosen the Varsity match ahead of Wales – and there was no way I was going to play along. I'm glad I did it though, as it brought my number of caps up to double figures.

One of our key players, Jonathan Davies, didn't play that well to be honest, and I was surprised with his attitude after the game. It didn't seem to matter to him that much that we had lost. Of course, as we later discovered, he had already agreed terms to go north to rugby league and that was probably why.

He wasn't the only player to go north in the months that followed, with the likes of John Devereux, Stuart Evans, Mark Jones, Jonathan Griffiths, Adrian Hadley, Alan Bateman and Paul Moriarty all turning their back on Welsh rugby for one reason or another. I resisted the temptation to join them. I suppose I should have gone and made one big killing and then come back, as I was still selling uPVC windows at the time. I had several offers but I had fallen for the woman who was to become my wife and I just didn't want to risk losing her.

*

The Romania game in fact wasn't the last time I played for Wales. As any true Ravens fan will tell you, that happened on 30 September 1989 when Bridgend hosted the national side at the Brewery Field and won! The date has been christened Blue Saturday by the Bridgend faithful!

It may seem strange today that Wales would play against a Welsh club side but the game had been arranged as a warm-up for the visit of New Zealand that November. It was quite a big deal as Wales didn't play many autumn internationals back then, nothing like today when you have a full set of four games.

Wales had already played against and beaten Newbridge – another game I played in for my country – the week before and we had a pretty much full-strength side on show. In hindsight it was a poor decision by the WRU as it was a no-win situation for Wales – if we won people would say, "Well, what do you expect, it was only a club side?" and if we lost, we would get a hammering in the press.

As you would expect, the Bridgend boys were well up for the game – there were a number of players who, just like myself a few seasons earlier, had points to prove after being overlooked by the Welsh selectors. There was a massive crowd, the Brewery Field must have been full to capacity, and it was a bit surreal playing for Wales in Wales against my own club!

Aled Williams, at outside-half, was just outstanding that day, Kevin Ellis was phenomenal but he was always 100 per cent. I remember Jeremy Cooper at seven had a storming game and so did Owain Williams – Bridgend had a great back row at the time. I was up against Richard Diplock, who was a good mate of mine. All of them had fantastic games, everyone played out of their skins and the wings had plenty of ball. It was amazing to see but I remember thinking, 'Why can't they play like that when I'm playing?'

The turning point came when Kevin Ellis, who had been knocking on the Welsh door for a while but, for whatever reason, was being ignored, caught Robert Jones at the back of a Welsh scrum and Buddy (Mike Budd) flattened him. Jeremy Cooper, who was everywhere that day, turned the ball over and broke through a maze of players to streak down the field before being tackled deep inside the Welsh 22 but was able to offload to Owain Williams, who in turn popped it up to Kevin to sprint under the posts. It was a brilliant try and, as he was running back, he was handed a water bottle and instead of taking a drink out of it he squirted the water up in the air and ran and caught it in his mouth! That just stuck with me. Always the showman.

The final score was Bridgend 24 Wales 17. It was strange as I was really glad for Bridgend that they had beaten Wales but I didn't have much of a game to be honest.

There were a few shouts of, "I bet you wish you were playing for Bridgend today, Webby!"

To be honest, I wouldn't have wanted Wales to beat Bridgend, even though I was playing for Wales. I was secretly quite glad. It was great for the club – beating the national side. Good on them, even if it did end my Wales career, as I never played for my country again after that.

*

I hadn't played for Wales for a while – it must have been 18 months since the Romania game – and I was aware that former internationals were given free tickets from the WRU to watch Wales's home games. I fancied going to watch one of the games, so I went along to the WRU offices in the Arms Park and asked them for a ticket. I was told by this woman, who worked there, that they don't just hand them out, you have to be a former international.

I said, "Well, I haven't played for 18 months so I am a former international."

"No," she said. "You have to formally retire."

"OK," I replied, "give me a piece of paper and a pen." And I wrote, 'I want to announce that from this moment, Glenn Webbe has officially retired from international rugby.'

Then I signed it and handed it over saying, "There you are, there's my official retirement from international rugby."

She hesitated and then said, "OK." And she handed me a pair of tickets. You had one free but were allowed to purchase the one next to you. I put the tickets safely in my pocket and headed to the door before stopping, turning, and saying to her, "I have some news for you, hot off the press."

"What's that?" she asked.

"I've just come out of retirement!" And I took off.

*

I never gave up hope of being picked to play for Wales again, even when someone faster than me came along in the shape of Nigel Walker. There was a lot of hype surrounding Nigel when he announced that he was switching to rugby and joining Cardiff. He was a top-class athlete who had competed in the semi-finals of the 110m hurdles at the 1984 Olympic Games in Los Angeles. While there was no doubting he had serious pace, a number of people were questioning whether he had the necessary skills to play rugby.

But I knew Nigel of old, and what a lot of people didn't realise was that he had a rugby background, having played in school. He was quick back then but only averagely quick. But when he went to the Olympics he had a flat time over 100m of around 10.4 seconds, which in rugby circles was phenomenal – remember, my fastest time was only 10.8!

He took to senior rugby like a duck to water because he was just carrying on from where he had left off at school. With all the athletics training, and weight training and body maintenance he had been doing as an athlete – they train in a completely different way to rugby players – he was in superb condition. As long as the grounds were firm and there was room to move and he had the ball in his hands, then nothing was going to touch him. He made a fantastic start and he was a very good player.

Needless to say, when Bridgend came to face Cardiff, there was a great deal of hype and expectation ahead of the game as we were to go head-to-head for the first time. The game was down at the Brewery Field, and he was lined up on the left wing, which was his favourite, and I was on the right. It was the first time that I had been up against someone who was obviously quicker than me. Most of the time the boot was on the other foot. I was to learn what people meant when they said to me that they would show me the outside and, nine times out of ten, I would take it! When your opposite number has more pace, there's nothing you can do.

Usually, when I ran at someone, I would try to run at them for as long as I could before veering out, so that they would be flat-footed or going from a standing start while I was already into my stride. They would then have to turn and by the time I'd got on their outside shoulder, I was away. That's the tactic I tried with Walker the first time I got the ball. I ran right at him and then veered away, got on the outside – I heard the cheer from the crowd – but within ten paces he had turned around and caught me from behind. That had never happened to me before.

I just thought, 'Wow!' The next time I tried a similar sort of thing – I stepped outside, veered out, then stepped in. He turned a complete circle while I was haring for the posts and the same thing happened again – he caught me from behind. He wasn't a technically sound tackler: he just jumped on my back, slid down my body and that was it.

Then came a clearance kick from Mike Rayer which didn't quite find touch. It went over my head and so I had to catch it with my back to the opposition. When I turned, there was

Walker just standing waiting for me with his arms stretched out on either side like a spider. As I have said before, time seems to go so slowly but, in reality, it happens so quickly. My thought process was, 'I've tried to go outside him and it didn't work. There's no point trying to go inside him and I'm not a very good kicker, even though a little chip over the top would be the best option.'

So there was only one thing for it and I set off! I tucked the ball into my body with my right hand, my shoulder dropped and my knees came up as my legs pumped – I just ran as hard as I possibly could. As I made contact, Walker dropped down, and I hit him with my shoulder as hard as I could and he just rolled over backwards as I ran over the top of him and between the posts and slammed the ball down for a match-winning try. As I turned and looked back, I saw the Cardiff sponge man was running onto the field. Walker ended up being stretchered off and I thought, 'Yes! There's only one currant in this bun!'

I have spoken to Nigel lots of time since – we are friends and his daughter, Abby, is the same age as my daughter, Lily, and they went to the same school. I even helped bring his brother Kevin to Bridgend at one time. He has mentioned the incident, and he was out for a couple of months afterwards with a problem with his AC joint after that non-tackle, but he did go on to play 17 times for Wales, so there was no lasting damage.

CHAPTER 10

Touring

SOMEONE TOLD ME once that Lawrence Dallaglio had quoted me in one of his books as saying, 'When I die, I don't want to go to heaven, I just want to go on a rugby tour.'

It's true. Touring was probably the best thing about playing rugby in the amateur era. I travelled the world in my time and that would never have been possible for a boy from Ely unless he had been pretty good at rugby.

When I played, almost every club, whatever the level, had an end-of-season tour, even if it was just a weekend away to Southend. Touring was even used as currency, the inducement when it came to poaching players. Approached players would ask, "Where are you going on tour at the end of the year?" You didn't get paid, but a lot of players joined clubs depending upon where they were going at the end of the season.

Touring was a great time, a really good time of my life. You see people stripped bare, in all forms of undress! It's like they say, "You have to live with someone to really get to know them." When you are away with the lads, on tour, it's so competitive to start with but then it just becomes a massive bonding exercise. Everyone who has played rugby would have experienced a tour and if you speak to any rugby player, anywhere in the world, they will understand – that's where the affinity, rugby player to rugby player, comes from. It's like a nod and a wink and you know what everyone else has gone through.

It was slightly different when touring with Wales – with

your club you already know the boys, so you know who the headcases are and what to expect and so on, from the off. When you toured with Wales there was a lot more discipline and you were training harder, so there was more to overcome. When you are new to the set-up, you know of the people who you are touring with but you don't really know them.

But on any tour you are still bonding a great deal and making friendships that you never really thought that you would; you change your opinion about people. You also find that some people are a lot better than you actually realised, fitter or more skilful, faster or stronger, better players, but there are also others who you think, 'Hang on, you're not all that you're cracked up to be.'

Even the drinking sessions are more organised. There is always a hierarchy and a kangaroo court, a lot of the same antics went on with Wales as with a club. It was still a case of what goes on tour with Wales, stays on tour with Wales.

I don't know what it's like now, with the professional era, perhaps it's just all hard work, but I'm sure that they do let their hair down at times and go through the same bonding process as we did and I'm sure that they always will.

*

I've had some great tours at all levels, from my youth days at Canton Rugby Club to going away with Wales. My first ever tour was to Benidorm, with Canton's senior team, when I was a fresh-faced and naïve 16 year old. There were two matches arranged and a few of us youth boys were invited along and played our first senior games despite not being old enough. It was a fantastic experience but most memorable because it was the first time I set eyes upon Sticky Vicky.

If you ask anyone who has been to Benidorm on a rugby tour, they should be able to tell you that Sticky Vicky is a stripper. She must have been touching 60 when I first saw her show but I'm told that she's still going strong – although it must be her daughter or something. It must be a legacy thing.

We were in this club knocking back the pints, as the senior players were trying to get the youngsters drunk, when the lights were dimmed and this voice came over the speakers, "Ladies and gentlemen, Sticky Vicky!"

Then this woman came out, wearing a big feather boa, and started taking her clothes off until she was left with just a pair of stilettos on. As a teenager who had never even seen a pornographic magazine – well, only one or two – I was gobsmacked. She then disappeared behind this screen, returned and picked a guy, told him to finish his drink and made him lie down and place the empty glass on his forehead. She then moved five feet away and popped this ping-pong ball out from below, as it were, and it landed in the glass! She would repeat the trick, with several guys lined up, and pop, pop, pop, she hit every glass. People were queuing up to be one of her stooges.

Her pièce de résistance was throwing darts out of there at a dartboard – I'm sure if you had asked her, she would have been able to throw a ball in to a lineout! I will never forget her.

*

It wasn't all good, however, and just as in life, there were highs and lows on any tour. By far the lowest point came in 1984 on one of my first tours with Bridgend. It was a fantastic trip to Ontario, Canada, a wonderful country but it turned out to be a bit of an eye-opener for me. We went to this place called Friday's Bar, all decked out in purple tank tops with 'Bridgend Canada Tour 1984' on them. Our number one dress code was the official club blazer; the tank tops were number two and then casual wear was number three. It was a Friday night and so the place was heaving.

There was a big crowd of us all standing in a circle, chatting away, when this chap, who must have been a local, just barged his way past. One of the boys, Richie Griffiths, said, "Don't you say excuse me around here?"

And he replied, "I don't say anything to you." Then he hit Richie with the bottom of his bottle. The best punch I have ever seen followed. Richie caught him so straight and hard it just hit this guy right back out of the circle. The whole place erupted after that and there was a big old bar fight like something out of the comedy cowboy film *Blazing Saddles*. After it died down we realised that, as we were just passing through, we had better be the ones to leave, so we all went outside. The problem was, the guys who had caused all the trouble came outside as well, and it all kicked off again.

Then this older guy, who turned out to be the father of one of the locals who was getting a tuning, entered the fray but caught a stray punch and hit the deck. He just lay there not moving. 'He's dead,' we all thought.

Then came the sound of police sirens and everyone scattered, apart from myself, as I was trying to revive this man on the floor. I put him in the recovery position and checked him for any signs of life. Fortunately, he started to come round and as the police approached he sat up, pointed to me and told the cops, "It was him!"

On went the handcuffs and I was thrown into the back of a patrol car and taken to the police station. I now have a criminal record in Canada because I was finger printed and appeared before a judge. While this was going on, so I'm told, the team had a big meeting about the fight and one of the senior players, Chris O'Callaghan, said, "Look, Glenn's locked up and it was nothing to do with him, so whoever the culprit is, just own up so we can get Glenn out of jail."

There must have been a circle of 30 players and they all looked at Richie Griffiths, who didn't flinch.

I was held in custody for a couple of days and while sat in that cell I scratched into the wall: 'The innocent will suffer for the violent – Glenn Webbe, 1984.'

If I ever get locked up again in Canada, I will have a look

to see if it's still there! They say that travel broadens your horizons and I certainly learned a valuable lesson, but it's all history now and just part and parcel of life. As I said, there have been lots of little lessons down the years – I must know everything, me!

*

A far more enjoyable trip to North America came along when Bridgend organised a tour to Atlanta in 1990. Our flight had been scheduled for the day after our defeat to Neath in the Schweppes Cup final so, after enjoying a good night out in Cardiff drowning our sorrows, it was back to the club in the morning and off to Heathrow.

Every side has a character who, let's say, would never qualify as a brain surgeon, if you know what I mean! Our prop, David Austin, however, would do well to become a hospital porter! I'm not being derogatory – I actually love Dai – but let me give you some examples.

That tour was the first time I met Dai. Wayne Hall had brought him down from Pencoed. He was a good player, very mobile, and would do whatever Halley told him. He believed in him completely. When Halley didn't play, Dai wasn't the same player, as he used to wind him up and get him going. So, when Halley said, "Webby, I've got someone here who will beat you in an arm wrestle," Dai had no doubt he would win.

He turned to Dai and said, "Dai, you will do him, won't you?"

"Yeah," said Dai.

"Come on then," I said, sighing. "Let's get this over and done with."

We went to the bar and clasped hands. Then I said, "Hold me for three seconds and I'll say you won."

"OK."

"Ready?"

Bam! It was all over. Basically he wasn't trying to push, he was just concentrating on holding me, so offered less resistance, giving me the edge.

Dai was shocked and spent the next few days just watching me. As the tour progressed, we were going into bars and, as I used to play a bit of pool up in Ely, I would chalk the cue just by holding the chalk on the tip and using my right foot to swivel the cue against my left foot. Dai was watching from across the room and, later on, I saw him try to mimic me and 'smash!', the cue would go flying to the ground. Also, as a kid, I got good at what we called Kung Fu sticks and could swivel them around my body, under my arm, around my head and snap them to a stop. It's one of those things that won't go away, just like riding a bike, so I started doing it with the pool cue in between shots.

Once again, Dai was watching and later on I saw him, out of the corner of my eye, trying to copy me before 'smash!' the cue clattered into his face! I don't know what world he was in but I was just watching him watching me, giggling to myself that he found me so fascinating.

As I said, I really liked Dai, although he was the butt of everyone's jokes, and we were roommates at one stage. He got so drunk once, he fell asleep and the boys shaved one of his eyebrows off. When we woke up the next morning he said, "Webby, look at what they've done."

"Don't worry about it Dai," I said. "That's what they are like. The best thing you can do is shave the other one off."

"Do you reckon?"

"Yeah," I said. "That way you won't look any different."

So he shaved the other one off!

"What do you think?" he asked me. I almost choked trying not to laugh out loud. He just looked so odd.

"Dai," I said. "I think you should try something else. I think you should draw them back in pen."

"Good idea," he said. "Have you got a pen?"

"Here you are," I said, and I handed him a blue one. He drew his eyebrows back in blue!

"That's it, Dai. Perfect."

I rushed down to the breakfast hall and said, "Quick boys, Dai is coming down. Don't say anything about his eyebrows!"

When Wayne Hall saw him, he just said, "Alright Dai?"

"Hi Wayne."

"Good night's sleep?"

"Yeah, thanks."

But behind his back the boys were struggling to keep it together – he looked like a tortoise.

Later in the tour he had a heart-to-heart with me and asked, "How did you beat me in that arm wrestle? You're only a winger but you're so strong."

"It's just life in Ely really," I said. "Growing up we'd have competitions for headbutting, kicking each other in the nuts, punching each other."

"You didn't?!"

"Yeah, yeah. We'd regularly have a punching each other in the stomach competition. Reckon you would beat me, Dai?"

"Yeah," he said.

So we went down to the bar and got the whole of the team around us.

"Go on then, who's going first?" I asked.

"I'll go first," he said.

"Go on then Dai, as hard as you want," I said.

"Really?"

"Yeah, really."

So he wound a punch up and hit me in the stomach but as I used to box a bit, I was easily able to absorb it without any real hurt.

"You can hit, Dai," I said, pretending to blow a bit.

"Was that hard?"

"Yeah, it really hurt," I said. "My go now."

He put his hands behind his back and I looked to see where his solar plexus was, turned and 'Bam!' I hit the sweet spot and he just doubled up letting out a loud groan.

"Dai? Dai?" I called, as he was on his knees still unable to stand. "It's your go."

He was on the floor for a good five minutes.

We were drinking together later on when he asked, "How did you do that?"

I shook my head and said, "I shouldn't really have done it as I have practised and practised for this. I stand in the doorway to my bedroom and slam the door into my stomach. I just breathe out when I do it."

"Oh, right," he said, and we just carried on with the night.

Much later, when I was going back to the room and reached the corridor, I heard what sounded like someone being whacked.

"Oomph!" Then there was a pause before "Oomph!" came again.

As I got to our room, there was Dai, in his underpants, at half-past-two in the morning, standing in the doorway, slamming the door into his stomach!

"That's the way Dai," I said, and edged past him and climbed into bed calling out, "Goodnight."

"Night Glenn. Oomph!"

He was just so gullible but great fun. I can't think of any dare that he wouldn't do. He was such a likeable guy.

*

Another common theme that almost everyone who has been on a rugby tour will know about is the kangaroo court. The official definition is one of a court that 'ignores recognised standards of law or justice', which is spot-on when it comes to rugby tours as it gives the senior players the opportunity to have a bit of fun at the expense of the accused, whether deserved or not. In this instance, the accused was one Scott Gibbs and the punishment was absolutely deserved.

At the time Gibbs was one of a handful of boys who had not long come up out of youth rugby, along with the centre

Stephen Pritchard and hooker Leighton Phillips. Even then he was a very good player, very strong but fairly small – I don't know how he managed to generate so much power. It was unbelievable to see people twice his size bouncing off him. I wasn't surprised when he went on to become a British & Irish Lions legend.

I was one of the senior players, along with Wayne Hall and Mike Budd. Those kids had no respect whatsoever. We were at this hotel and they were making a hell of a racket, jumping off the top of changing huts into the pool, causing mayhem. Then, one of them thought it would be funny to introduce a floater into the pool. It wasn't. The pool had to be cleared and drained and they spoilt the fun for everyone.

The management complained and we were asked to find out who the culprit was. So, the next day at breakfast, us senior players made a point of sitting next to the table of kids – as we called them – and I said, just loud enough to be overheard, to Halley, "Yesterday was so funny. Someone put a floater into the pool. They had to get everybody out. It was hilarious. I wish I had thought of that."

A little while later someone nudged me and I heard Gibbs whispering excitedly, "Webby, you were on about the pool, it was me. I did it!"

"Right!" I said, "You little b******, we've got you."

We made him apologise but that wasn't just it, we had him up in front of a kangaroo court at the end of the tour. Everyone got penalised and punished, that's the whole idea of them, but Gibbs was in for special treatment.

Mike Budd, who was the prosecutor, called him up and the charges were read out.

"You are accused of defecating in a public swimming pool. How do you plead? Guilty or not guilty?"

"Not guilty." A quick bang to the head soon changed his plea.

He was stripped down to his pants and he was blindfolded.

Then a bucket of water, with a floater in it, was placed at his feet.

"Check that blindfold Halley," instructed Buddy. As he did so he deliberately allowed Gibbs to look down and see the disgusting sight below. What he didn't know was that we had another bucket with a peeled banana floating in it, which was later substituted for the original.

"Right Gibbs," said Buddy. "There's a bucket on the floor, reach your hand down."

"No! I'm not doing that," he cried.

"What do you mean no? Have you been peeping?"

"No, no," he said.

"Well, reach your hand down and feel around."

He did as he was told and made all these squeamish noises as he did so.

"Can you feel it?"

He was as squeamish as a vegan in an abattoir!

"Pick it up and eat it!"

"'Nooooo!" he cried.

"Webby," Buddy called out. "Do it for him!"

"My pleasure," I said.

Two of the other boys grabbed him and I rammed a peeled banana in his chops! He spluttered and screamed until the realisation set in and he shouted, "You buggers!"

It was only at the time of writing this book that it came to light that Scott Gibbs had been innocent all along and had chosen to own up to protect his friend Stephen Pritchard, who was the real culprit. Pritch had begged Gibbsy to take the rap as he was on his last warning and feared being booted out. "They love you," he had reasoned, "and would never drop you." As a matter of fact, Pritch had also provided the floater for the kangaroo court – he probably had a problem.

*

Another tradition of touring, or away trips, was the initiation ceremonies. They were an opportunity to welcome new players into the fold and do a bit of teambuilding by humiliating them – but in a good way, like guys do to the groom on his stag do.

Mine came on my first stay away with Bridgend. It was a fixture against Coventry, who used to be one of the English first-class sides, and it was decided by the senior players that I would be initiated. I remember that the Human League were number one at the time with 'Don't you want me?' I used to love that song and sang it on the bus on the way up.

I had bought a nice outfit especially for the night out, it was all burgundy – burgundy shoes with black piping, really baggy burgundy trousers that came right in around the ankles, a nice burgundy shirt with a button-down collar with black buttons – I really thought that I looked the part. Unfortunately, the likes of Meredydd James had other plans for my look and they decided to pin me down and spray my hair silver – it took weeks for it to all come out fully.

I didn't resent my treatment in the least – it's got to be done. When you are being initiated, you know that you're not going to come to any real harm, although, it is awkward at the time. You get embarrassed, but you don't get hurt to any great degree. It's all part of bonding as a team. When you come out the other end you can't wait for it to be your turn to initiate someone else.

*

I loved touring so much I even went on tour with Neath! My best mate Robbie joined Neath later in his career and was going on about how much fun it was down there, that they were so gullible and that he was the kiddie. I wanted to see this for myself and, as Neath were going across to Ireland on a short tour at the same time Wales were playing out in Dublin, Robbie managed to get me on the trip.

I knew some of the Neath players really well, like Stuart Evans and Dai Joseph, from my time with Wales Youth so I soon settled in. Dai Joseph's party piece was a fly circus. We were in this ancient bar when he turned to me and said, "Webby, have you ever heard of a flea circus?"

"Yeah," I said.

"Well I have something similar but with flies."

"Get out of here."

"I'll show you." Now, there were three or four flies buzzing around one of the pub's light bulbs and Dai walked up and started beckoning with his finger. "Come on my lovelies," he encouraged. "Come with me." And as he started walking away, the flies followed him! I couldn't believe what I was seeing. He led them to another light bulb on the other side of the room. I was dumbfounded.

"How on Earth did you do that?" I asked.

"I can't tell you," he said.

"Come on Dai! You have got to tell me, it's brilliant."

"No, it's a secret."

He wouldn't relent until finally, at the end of the night, I had worn him down and he gave in. However, when he told me where he had put his finger to be able to draw the flies, I knew that I would never repeat the trick!

The Neath boys took touring to a new level. Their main game was to try to get down the aisle to the back of the bus while everyone else did their best to stop you, without leaving their seats, but they would bombard you with all sorts.

They knew that I liked to arm wrestle so I had to take on Stuart Evans. After I beat him, I had to take on Kevin Phillips and I did him. Then Dai Joseph – I beat them all until there was only Brian Williams, the farmer, left.

"You won't beat me, man," he said in his west Wales accent. He was just a naturally strong person who could pick up a sheep under each arm.

"Come on, have a go," I said. So, he sat down. We were locked together, just holding and holding each other. He was really strong, I had finally met my match. So I said, "This is so tough. Robbie, give me the special coin."

And Robbie passed a normal pound coin over to my free hand and I held it up to my forehead and pressed it in and started chanting, "I need the power of Zeng. I need the power of Zeng." I was just trying to take his attention away – anything to beat him.

"Come on then, Bri," I said, before repeating in a voice like Darth Vader, "Zeng. Zeng. Zeng."

With each "Zeng" my arm got further and further down until I let out one final "Zeng!" and beat him.

"For fecks sake!" he cried and stormed off, shaking his head.

"He's done you Brian, he's done you!" the boys shouted.

"It wasn't Webby," he shouted. "It was that fecking Zeng bloke it was!"

He always insisted I had used the power of Zeng, otherwise I would never have beaten him.

*

One of my last tours came after I had retired from first-class rugby but it was still one of the best as it saw me getting a call from the British & Irish Lions – well the veteran equivalent, that is. I had been invited to play for a British Lions veterans' side in a tournament out in Bermuda, along with Alan Martin, Stuart Evans, Mark Ring and Mike Budd, and we managed to reach the final against the New Zealand veterans. The talk turned to how we were going to face the haka – all teams must discuss it amongst themselves before going out – and I said, "Just listen to what I've got to say because it's the best possible way to respond."

"What are you going to do, Webby?"

"Just follow my lead."

"OK."

So, after the haka the guy on the public address system said,

"I think there's going to be a response to the haka from the British Lions led by Glenn Webbe."

The New Zealanders lined up just by the halfway line and I walked out to face them, just five metres away, with the rest of my side lined up in a semicircle behind me. I stomped my left foot forwards and let out a loud "Arrrg!" and the boys behind me did the same thing. Then I moved my left foot back and let out another "Arrrg!"

Then I repeated the sequence shouting, "You put your left foot in, you put your left foot out, in, out, in, out and shake it all about!" The whole of the crowd erupted with laughter. The look on the All Blacks' faces was just like thunder. They were not impressed in the least but I had finally been able to stage a comeback to their haka and restore the balance! They jeered – they didn't show any respect for us! It was our haka and we weren't allowed to go after theirs. They gave us completely no respect at all.

After the game they were brilliant but as for the game itself, they just flip that switch and they don't give you anything. Everything they have is left on that field. They had the likes of Smoking Joe Stanley, John Gallagher and Terry Wright in their side and I got tackled by them all.

It was a good game. I was around 36 years old and still fit and training hard, so I gave it a good old go when I got the ball and played quite well. As for the result, we didn't do too badly, we lost but only by two tries to nil – they wouldn't take kicks at goal as it was against their ethic of running everything.

*

The game had gone professional by then and, while players had got better, the training had become tougher and tougher at the expense of much of the enjoyment – at least from where I was watching. That tour served as a timely reminder of what the game used to be all about. There was nothing really on the tournament and everybody was back in the amateur zone. It reminded us of the fun that we used to have and by the end of that trip we were singing songs and playing drinking games – it reminded me why I stayed in love with rugby. We had all started from the same humble beginnings and been amateur players once upon a time. It was the fun and camaraderie that kept us in the game. I realised that, as I climbed up the rugby ladder, there seemed to be less fun and more hard work.

CHAPTER 11

Sevens

THE SEVENS CIRCUIT came at the start of the season, in
August, and we used to use it to get fit for the 15-a-side season.
I used to love playing sevens when I was younger. There were
tournaments all over the place and, if I was given the ball in
space, having good pace, all I had to do was run the tries in.
I knew a few songs and beer games for afterwards, so I really
enjoyed it. It was always a good craic.

My first taste of a major tournament came while I was still
in youth rugby and was asked to play for an invitation side
called Steepholm. They were a pretty good outfit and entered
a lot of big tournaments such as the Aberaeron Sevens, which
was pretty big in its day, and the Amsterdam Sevens, which
was always the pinnacle – apart from the Hong Kong Sevens
of course but that was practically a world cup. Amsterdam, to
a young kid, was like another world; all these teams from all
over the place, playing in a tournament that lasted nearly a
whole week, it was as big as it got. I fell in love with the game
from the start.

I probably enjoyed sevens more than I enjoyed the 15-a-side
game. Individual games are over much quicker but you have
a whole tournament with at least five games – ten if it was a
two-day affair. It's got so much drama involved and so much
happens in a short space of time – it can change so quickly, it's
fast and exciting. It's only seven minutes each way but it's so

intense, so concentrated. I'm sure it equates to more ball-in-hand time than any 15-a-side game.

*

In one early tournament, which took place in England somewhere, I was playing for a team put together with the backing of this money man called Tony Clemo, who was the then Cardiff City chairman. We made it to the semi-final without playing too well, and Tony arrived in a helicopter and said in his team talk, "If you win this tournament boys, I will give you £100 each."

That was an unbelievable amount of money back then and it was the first time I started to think seriously about the impact of professionalism because we went on to win the tournament. I wasn't sure if the money on offer made me play any better but it started us out on the road to success.

That experience also started me off on the road to setting up my own sevens outfit which I entered in tournaments up and down the country. We always had the nucleus of the same side, which was packed with fantastic players. There was David Bishop, who was outstanding at sevens, Gary Peace, one of the best at pulling the strings, the ridiculously talented Mark Ring, Paul Turner was another regular, Gerald Cordle and myself usually provided the pace on the wing – there were also a number of players who weren't great 15-a-side players but were superb at sevens.

We became quite recognisable because we always had a large entourage with us and we always did very well and used to win more than we lost. On one trip, to the British Heart Foundation Sevens up in Moseley, as we were arriving, a little bit late, some English lag, with his tweed jacket and green wellington boots said, "Oh no! Those bloody Welshmen are here again." That made me giggle and so, when I went to register, and was asked for the name of our team, I said, "The Bloody Welshmen!"

The guy looked at me and then wrote down 'The Welshmen' and that's how the name came about. It stuck. We won that tournament beating Fiji in the final. They even had Waisale Serevi playing for them. It was amazing.

A guy called Ian Brice, who was involved with the Crawshays and owned an insurance company, helped us set up initially and sponsored our jerseys. The Welshmen went from strength to strength after that. We were a very noticeable side, not least for the kit we wore, which I had designed myself. While playing in Amsterdam I noticed that the grounds were so hard you would pick up grass burns on your hips and below your shorts – these were the days of short shorts! By day two your glands would come up because your body was trying to fight off the infection and you wouldn't be able to run properly or make the team – and not because of the drinking the night before! So, I designed a pair of shorts that began above the hips and came right down to the knees – we looked like something out of the 19th century but they did the job.

I even designed a Welshmen badge made up of a player with one half in a suit and tie and the other half in rugby kit. The Hs in The Welshmen were rugby posts. All our kit was branded with a FAFFA logo, which stood for f*** all for f*** all!

We used to do a lot on and off the field through the success of The Welshmen. I got asked to do a lot of after-dinner speaking but I used to shy away from it. They would push me and I would tell them that I would look for a replacement, and so I would ask players like Jiffy (Jonathan Davies), Mark Ring or Robert Jones if they would like to do it, and I would take a cut! It all helped to keep the show on the road.

Top players were queuing up to play for The Welshmen and I was often spoilt for choice. There was one occasion though, where it turned sour, as Dai Bryant was so unfortunate as to pick up a career-ending injury. I really do feel guilty about the fact that the last time he played rugby at a high level was for The Welshmen. I had begged him to play when he didn't really want to and he suffered cruciate knee ligament damage. He never fully recovered.

One of the most memorable Welshmen outings was a bank holiday weekend tournament we played up in Newcastle upon Tyne. Sir John Hall hadn't long taken over Newcastle and there was beginning to be some decent money in the game. We had won the Caldy Sevens the day before, up on Merseyside, and had shared £5,000 in prize money. It was fantastic.

We had a brilliant squad, packed with Bridgend players including the likes of Owain Williams, Jason Forster, Andrew Williams, Matthew Lewis, Gareth Thomas, Dafydd James, Ian Greenslade and me. We had also attracted a sponsor, some landed English businessman who wanted us to do the rounds, visit a school and go to bed early – but that didn't happen. We were there to play rugby and that's it. I think he expected a more English type professional outfit but we were the opposite of that, but could still play a bit of rugby.

Newcastle were in one side of the draw and Northampton were in the other and, while it wasn't fixed, it became obvious that the organisers, led by Newcastle's director of rugby, Rob Andrew, wanted the two to meet in the final. We were just some also-rans but were putting 30 or 40 points on teams; we were playing some fantastic stuff.

We reached the semi-finals but had lost some players. Now the tournament's rules said that if you needed a replacement, and another team had already been eliminated, then you could use one of their players – I know this because we asked an official. Cardiff were up there but had been knocked out so we borrowed their winger, Steve Ford, and beat Northampton to reach the final. Our sponsor was over the moon; we had put his company on the map, and he took back everything he had said about us being a bunch of wasters.

As we waited to take the field for the final, they announced on the tannoy that there would be a 15-minute delay. Then this official came up to us and told us that we had been disqualified. They then put out another announcement saying that, due to the use of an ineligible player, The Welshmen were taking no further part in the tournament. They said that it was because we had played Steve Ford when he wasn't eligible.

I said, "You're joking. We cleared it with you before picking him."

"No you didn't," said the official. I couldn't believe it and called him out as an absolute liar.

We were gutted, not so much because we were being told that we couldn't play in the final, but because there was £10,000 in prize money on offer for the winners and £5,000 for the runners-up.

Now, we had our kit bags with us, as we had planned a quick getaway straight after the game, and I came up with an idea.

"Come on boys," I said, "follow me."

"We're going home then, are we?" they asked.

"No," I said. "If we're not going to be in the final, then there's not going to be a final. We're going to sit in protest on the halfway line."

And we all walked out to the centre of the field and sat down with our kit bags – good old Jane Veysey who led that strike back in my schooldays would have been proud of me! The official just stared at us and then walked over and said, "I'm going to call the police."

"Go on then," I replied, and he stormed off. By then, the large crowd had noticed our protest and a slow hand-clap began to ring out around the ground.

'Oh dear,' I thought, 'the crowd are turning on us now.' But we had been playing such good rugby, the crowd were on our side. The next thing we knew, they started chanting, "Let them play! Let them play!"

Then, all the la-di-das in the hospitality marquees came running onto the field, with their G&Ts in hand, and sat down forming a huge circle around us in support. Eventually the organisers came over and said, "OK, there's been a mistake but you have to abide by the decision."

"But there's at least £5,000 at stake here," I said.

They had a little conflab and came back and said, "If we give you the £5,000, will you go home?"

I said, "Yes."

"OK. Will you come off now?"

"I've got a better idea," I said. "Why don't you go and get the money first?"

They went to get the money and counted it out, there and then on the field, and we left with a lap of honour with the crowd cheering. The only downside was Northampton, who we had dusted in the semi-final, beat Newcastle in that final so we could have doubled our money making it a very profitable weekend. Needless to say, we weren't invited back the following year but we won the Henley Sevens instead and that also had a £10,000 prize.

*

I owe a lot to sevens and I'm not envious of the players on the sevens circuit today – it's just like everything else, the game has changed so much. Tactically, it used to be quite a lateral game where you tried to create space. I worked out the main ways of winning the ball are: in the air from kick-offs and lineouts, from knock-ons and scrums, or through turnovers in contact and at rucks or mauls.

I would always pick a big forward for kick-offs and lineouts, always a clever fat controller type hooker in the middle, who didn't do a lot of the running but was a general and could give the orders and create space for others. Then I would have players who could exploit that space and make the most of the opportunities. We always tried to simplify the game and just get big men to run at small men and fast men to run at slow men, to try to create a mismatch all the time.

In those early days there were a couple of tournaments where I was up against some seriously quick players, who were at least as quick as myself. I played against Tony Underwood and Martin Offiah a couple of times, and everyone, including myself, wanted to know if I was quicker than them, so I would try to take them on. My ego ruled my head in the early days – sometimes I beat them, sometimes I didn't.

As I got older, I realised that although the crowd might have wanted to know who was going to win those foot races, if I didn't win, I would get tackled and probably lose the ball. So a lot of the time I wouldn't take on someone who was possibly as quick as me. Instead, I would wander out of position, into the middle of the field, and take the ball on against someone who I knew didn't have my pace, like a fat controller, who I could easily beat. All I would have to do was run ten yards as fast as I could and they would give up the chase. I wouldn't look to run the length of the field, just a short burst past the slower players on the field. At least that's how I ended my career, looking for players I could still bully with my speed.

In the modern game nearly all the players are picked to try and break the game. There's much more contact in sevens now. It's a lot more brutal and tougher than it was. It's not such an art form any more.

Knowing what to do in sevens used to be as important as being able to do those things. We were talking after a game a while back, about just how important that sevens knowledge was. The argument rumbled on and someone pointed out that there was the Old Penarthians Sevens coming up and suggested we put our money where our mouth was and put a side together. This was about ten years ago, when we were all in our 40s, so we called ourselves The Way Over 40s. Unfortunately, when our jerseys came back it was spelt The Weigh Over 40s.

Our team included Jason Forster, Ian Greenslade, Adrian Durstan and Kevin Ellis. The ball shot out of a scrum in one match and Kevin couldn't even bend down so he put his foot under it and toed it to the outside-half's hands. We were a good team – 15 years before, we would have been world beaters. Despite our advanced years, we went all the way to the final and met The Emerging Ospreys. They needed extra time to beat us!

*

I loved the sevens game. I think it's a fundamental part of a player's education. Robert Howley even said that he got the confidence and ability to play for Wales through sevens. When you are a scrum-half or sweeper playing sevens and come up against named pacemen, and you are catching them from behind, or leaving them for dead, it does so much for your confidence. You can't always do that in 15s as it's too cluttered. But you can easily make a name for yourself in sevens. And he did. He was a phenomenal player.

Sadly, I never did make it out to Hong Kong. Although I have got a Honk Kong Sevens programme at home with my name in it – unfortunately it is crossed out, with Arthur Emyr written in instead.

CHAPTER 12

Calling it a day

I NEVER DID call time on my career with Wales and you never think, at the time, that any game is your last game for Wales. I was involved in a couple of squad sessions after the Romania game but never made the team or the bench. Ron Waldron had taken over from John Ryan, who I think jumped before he was pushed, after a hammering by England at Twickenham in February 1990. Neath were beating everyone at the time, so, as their coach, Ron was the obvious choice to take over but it was a heavily biased Welsh side – I think they even tried to switch to black jerseys!

Before one game we had a final training session in Sophia Gardens – it was always a fartlek session under Waldron – and Paul Thorburn tried to run through a crowd of players and ran smack into one of the trees that ringed the pitches. After Ron had announced the team, he handed over the floor to anyone who wanted to say something. My hand went up, as usual, and he said, "Oh, OK." He may have thought that I was going to be a bit controversial.

I stood up and said, "I'm gutted that I'm not playing but you can't fault the selection of Ieuan, he's the best wing in the country at the moment, but at 15... I would have probably gone with the tree that knocked Thorby out."

*

I was only 26 years old, and without knowing it, I had played my last game for Wales. I was just entering my prime and went on to play eight more seasons of first-class rugby. I never gave up hope and continued to play against the best wings in Wales and, more often than not, got the better of them but the call never came. I suppose it didn't help when Ieuan Evans became captain for a then record 22 games – but I still wasn't a left wing! Ron did have a chat with me about playing on the left wing, as Ieuan was also in the squad, but I replied, "Why doesn't Ieuan switch wings?" I admit that the younger me was a bit cheeky at times. I had already played for Wales on the left but I really didn't like playing there and decided to make a stand.

I added, "Ron, if you asked me to play prop or second row or hooker, I would play anywhere you asked for my country, but I would play like a right wing because that's what I am."

Ieuan actually started off in the centre. I remember the first time I saw him – we played in the same team in a Crawshays game. He came on and had a fantastic game, he really looked the part. They eventually moved him out to the wing because, basically, anyone outside of him never saw the ball as he would just tuck it under his arm and off he'd go. He was definitely one to watch.

We were rivals but I really got on with him off the field. He was a great fella, a really good character. I liked Ieuan a lot. There was no animosity with any of the players, just a healthy rivalry because everyone wanted to play. It wasn't like it is today, when everyone gets to play a part in the game – if you weren't picked to start then you were just a dirt tracker. I was often one of those and you would just become so disruptive – you would try to take your opposite number's head off in training. You would fly in with the tackles. In the end the coaches would take you out of it and tell you to calm down. It was only training but to you it was someone else wearing your jersey and you wanted to physically take it off them there and then.

I also got on with Ron Waldron, as much as you can get on with any coach as a player, but I did feel that he had bracketed me, Ringo and David Bishop together as a group of Cardiff troublemakers. It is unbelievable that Bishop only had one cap for Wales. He was worth 50 caps without a shadow of a doubt. He had immense confidence, immense ability and there was no doubt in his mind about what he was going to do and what he was going to achieve – I really did feel for him. How the regime could just shut people out when it's nothing to do with ability, I just don't know. In my opinion it was purely personal and was one of the biggest travesties of justice in Welsh rugby. I'd played with him in various teams and in sevens and played against him loads of times, and he was the ultimate competitor.

I got on really well with Robert Jones, who was always picked ahead of Bish-Bash (as I called him), and he was a class scrum-half but Bishop offered something different. There was a Cup game once between Pontypool and Swansea in Pontypool Park when Bish-Bash had the game of his life. He just picked Rob up a couple of times and pepper-potted him. He kicked an enormous drop-goal which clinched the game and did a little dance, holding one finger on each hand up in the air and waving that big backside of his from side to side – he's not a great mover but it underlined the point!

*

I went on to play eight more seasons for Bridgend and saw several future stars come through during a successful era for the club. Certainly one of the best was Robert Howley who, as a Bridgend boy, joined his local club in 1988. At the time our backs coach was Geoff Davies, who was a great coach in my opinion, his enthusiasm was infectious. It may have been a simple adjustment that he wanted you to make but if you did it and it worked, he would come back to you like a child at Christmas, he was so excited by it. It made you want to please him.

He was very analytical. I understand that he had helped develop Robert Jones – he was his PE teacher at Cwmtawe

Comprehensive School in the Swansea Valley – and he used to spend a lot of time with Robert Howley. Although Rob was young, he had a really good rugby mind and he wanted to know everything about the game. If there was someone who wasn't on the same intellectual rugby plane as him, he would get bored easily but he used to spend ages with Geoff, analysing things. It was no surprise that Rob would go on to become a brilliant coach himself.

Geoff was meticulous with his preparation and used to make notes for individual players before each game. On one occasion, a very windy day, he was going around everyone, explaining their role. When he came to me, he spoke about my alignment and positional play being important and that "the wind was a big factor".

I stopped him and said, "Who is he?"

Geoff looked at me and said, "What?"

I repeated, "Who is he?"

"Who's who?"

"The wing. You said that the wing was a big fat ****."

He just gave a loud exasperated sign, shook his head and moved on to the next player. I thought it deserved a laugh at least and, to be fair, a few years later he told me he had thought it was funny.

*

Another player who I had the privilege of seeing come through the Bridgend ranks was Gareth Thomas. Alfie came to us as a centre but he played on the wing as well. He was very quick and was a good long-distance runner too. At the start of the season you have your pre-season training where you get your fitness levels up and it would include sprinting 100, 200 and 400m and mile runs, and Alfie was always out in front. He was like a horse, he wouldn't get tired – you would have to shoot him in the end. He was a phenomenal athlete.

One game stands out in my mind in particular. It was the

1994–95 season and against Llanelli. Alfie was in the centre with John Devereux and they were up against Nigel Davies and Simon Davies. Alfie had a phenomenal game – he was the best centre on the field. We were talking about his future afterwards and I said, "I think you are going to play for Wales."

He said, "Shut up, Webby."

So I said, "How do you think you played today?"

"All right," he replied.

I said, "I think you outshone Devs today."

He said, "Perhaps."

"How do you think you went against Nigel? And what about Simon Davies?" The other centres were in the Welsh squad at the time and Alfie wasn't. "You're going to play for Wales before the end of the year."

"Yeah. Yeah."

"I'll bet you £100."

"OK," he said.

He was called up to the World Cup squad later that year and scored five tries against Japan in the first game. I sent him a telegram before the game – there were no mobile phones back then – that said, 'I told you. You owe me £100.'

When he came back after the World Cup he approached me during his first training session back, and said, "Here you are, Webby." And he gave me £100. I didn't take the money, because it wasn't a fair bet – I just believed in him so much. It was really nice to see someone coming through. When you are young you just don't know how good you are.

*

There was another side to Alfie, which I would never have predicted though – his being gay. I had better start at the beginning. The last game of the season was coming up and we always planned something big to mark the end of another year. On this particular occasion, as we were playing up in Ebbw Vale, we decided to stop off in Cardiff on the way home for a night out. We had food and went on a bit of a pub crawl and ended up in this new nightclub that had just opened, called Minsky's, which, as it turned out, was a drag bar and attracted the gay crowd. We didn't mind a bit, it was such a novelty, it was brilliant. There were acts and transvestites on the stage singing and dancing, teasing the boys, it was really funny. We weren't there to judge or make fun of anyone, we were there, like everyone else, to have a good time.

When I got home Sally asked where we had ended up and, when I told her, adding how much fun the place was, she wanted to see for herself. So the following Saturday I took Sally along and it was another great night. I didn't put two and two together at the time but we bumped into Alfie while we were there – he said the same story as me: he had had so much fun he decided to take his mates there. I didn't have a clue.

Now Greenslade and I used to enjoy starting rumours in the club – which always started with us saying, "Don't say nothing..." to see how long they took to get back to us. We would make things up such as, "Don't say nothing, but Robert Howley's going to Cardiff." Then, around ten minutes later, we would be in the bar and Wayne Barrington – Bridgend's superfan – would come up to us and say, "Have you heard about Howley?!" And we would just giggle to ourselves.

So, during the next training session when one of the boys asked me what I did on the weekend, I said, "I took Sally to Minsky's," followed by, "Look, don't say nothing now. Alfie was in there with his boyfriend!"

"You're joking?!" And that started the rumour off.

A couple of weeks later people were saying, "Guess what?"

"What?"

"Gareth Thomas is gay!"

I would just laugh as I knew – as far as I was concerned – that I had started that rumour. But it went on and on. Around a year later I went to an international game in Cardiff and I noticed some idiots were shouting abuse at Alfie, calling him gay. I jumped right in and shouted, "He's not!" I defended him like nobody's business, saying, "You're wrong! This is how it all started..." and I told them the story.

I told Greenslade, "We've created a monster here Compo, this is ridiculous. We've got to try and stop this rumour because it's gathering speed." It was even in the newspapers!

Then, not long after I'd finished playing, I had a phone call from Greenslade and he said, "I'm out with Alfie and he wants a word with you," and he put him on.

"Yeah," Alfie said, "those rumours are true. I am gay. I've got a boyfriend."

"Are you serious?" I asked.

"Yeah," he said sheepishly. "I just didn't know what you would say or how you would react. I asked Compo to tell you but he said I should do it."

"I'm astounded," I said, "not by the fact that you are gay, there's nothing wrong with that whatsoever, it's just that I have to start another rumour now, telling people that you're straight!" And that was it. We were as close, and remain as close, as ever.

I think he handled the whole coming out process perfectly – it can't be an easy situation for anyone to find themselves in but more so when you are in the public eye as much as Alfie is. When you look at what he's done since, it's amazing: he's set himself apart and has encouraged so many others to just be themselves.

*

Dafydd James came along at the same time as Alfie but that was down to a mix-up – Bridgend were after his older brother Stuart! Bridgend had sent a scout down to watch Kenfig Hill play and to approach Stuart James but, unbeknown to the scout, Stuart wasn't playing although his brother was. Afterwards the scout asked someone, "Is that James by there?" When they said yes, he went up to Dafydd and said, "Come along to training with Bridgend," thinking he was addressing his older brother.

And Dafydd said, "Alright!" He jumped at the chance.

Dafydd was a forced player really. He was good-paced but not lightning-quick and a good player, but not brilliant. He was determined, however, and fit and keen – he trained and trained and trained and forced his way in. In the end he was a very good player, which shows what dedication and determination can do. Ability is only part of it. The rest of it is all about resolution. You have got to have the willingness to work hard, you really do have to want it – you need to need it, to be honest with you.

Mark Ring used to train quite hard but he was more capable than most people could hope to be; there was a lot of natural ability there. I know for a fact that I didn't have a lot of natural ability but I knew that I was quick and I trained to be quicker. I knew that I was strong and I trained to be stronger. I was relatively elusive, but footballing wise, I wasn't a great kicker of the ball, and I did mishandle the ball once or twice! I'm aware of that and I tried to make up for it in other ways – to be as fit as I possibly could be and to be determined.

*

I had a little brush with show business in 1993 when I made an appearance on *Gladiators*. It started off as a programme for American TV – I still stay up late at night watching stupid programmes – and I was a big fan of the show. You had contestants from the public up against these huge bodybuilders and they were duffed up. I thought it was great fun, great viewing. Then it came over to this country and I thought, 'I'd love to go on that.'

I was supposed to be playing baseball one weekend that summer in Cardiff but the game was called off at the last minute. However, I saw a poster advertising auditions for *Gladiators* up in Llanrumney sports hall – it was meant to be.

I decided to go in and have a little look and the boys egged me on to give it a go. There were a few tests you had to complete in order to qualify – run 800m on a treadmill in under two minutes, which I did easily, then climb a rope up to the ceiling of the Dutch barn twice – the first time it was hands only and the second time you could use your legs as well. Again I did it easily. Only four of us passed, one was an ex-boxer called Mervyn Bennett, who I knew, and the two others I didn't know.

We were then given those pugil sticks, which the gladiators used to hit and prod each other, shaped like a big broom handle with a big foam weight at each end. They drew a little arena, around six foot in diameter, and you had to hit your opponent out of bounds. I was up against Mervyn, who was shorter than me but aggressive. Being heavier and with a longer reach, I just kept jabbing him with the end of the stick. He tried to blast me, but in the end I hit him out of the circle. They told me that I had qualified and that the TV show would be shot in five months' time, so to keep myself fit.

Just before I was due to go on we played a game against Llanelli and I had a massive whack on my leg and burst a quadricep. It became a race against time to be fit for the programme. I was hobbling around the place so I asked if I could come on at a later date. I was told if I didn't turn up I would have to reapply the following year. So I decided to go ahead, and ended up doing it practically on one leg. I didn't do terribly well.

I didn't regret it as it was good fun, and I got to meet Ulrika Jonsson and John Fashanu. He came up to me and said, "Aruga!"

I looked at him and said, "Where's that come from mate?"

"You have got to say 'aruga' back to me," he said, "It's my catchphrase."

It never caught on. It was never appropriate and he could never fit it into the show.

The whole episode was a bit embarrassing so I never told anyone that I was going – I didn't even tell my family, apart from Sally, who came up to the NEC in Birmingham for filming with me for the weekend. I just snuck up there and was glad that I had done so after failing so miserably. But the boys saw it, of course. As soon as I turned up at the next training session all I heard was, "Gladiators ready!?"

For a while after that, I would be playing a game and someone in the crowd would shout out, "Gladiators ready. Webby, ready!?" I used to have a little bit of a giggle to myself. I had that for a couple of seasons. At least I was on it, and it was harder than it looks on TV. It was tough.

*

I told Bridgend that I planned to finish at the end of the 1995–96 season – I was 35 years old, had given the club 14 seasons, playing 422 games and scoring 286 tries, so I had put in a good shift and the time just seemed right. John Phelps was our coach at the time, although by the end it just seemed that there was a new coach every half-hour – even Clive Norling (the Nineties equivalent of Nigel Owens) became our coach at one stage! It was an idea, which they thought was a good one to start with. But knowing the rules of the game inside out, and being able to argue with the referee doesn't make you a better side. And from the start, all the referees were against us because we had Norling at the helm!

He wasn't in sole charge. He was there with Steve Fenwick, and it was always a case of, who was in charge? They were both directors of rugby and both had a say. There was no cohesion, it just didn't work. Neither of them was a tried and tested coach and Dai Bryant ended up doing most of the coaching. It didn't work.

*

I think it's the case with most professional sports people, whether rugby players, football players or boxers, that the ambition goes before your ability. I suppose that's what keeps you safe. If you were a boxer and you'd lost all of your ability but still had the ambition, then you would get seriously hurt. I think it's a gradual thing, where you tend to want it less and less. You can see the hardships, 'Oh no, training tonight. Here we go again!', or when you have to chase back when you know you should have had that ball, you think, 'What's the point?' Or you blame somebody if a pass isn't perfect. Little things start creeping into your psyche and the game gets less and less appealing – you can still do it, but you just don't want it as much. Injuries take longer to recover from and you are quite happy when you are injured sometimes. And it's easier to say what you could have done than actually going out there and proving it.

It just got to a stage where I thought, 'time is up'. I still played a load of games afterwards – charity games and for invitation sides – and still ran the length of the field and felt good but there was no pressure to do anything, it wasn't really competitive.

My last competitive game for Bridgend was away to Pontypool at the end of the 1995–96 season. After a shower and getting changed, I thought to myself, 'this is it, it's the end. I've had a good old innings.' It was difficult to realise that it had all come to an end.

*

I'm not one of those players who claims his generation was the best. I would love to play today. Definitely. I'm also glad that I played when I played and I would have liked to have played before I played too. I would have liked to have experienced as much about rugby as I could. The game was just becoming professional as I was finishing and for my generation the biggest struggle was the financial one – you had to give things up to play the game at such a high level. You had expenses but you couldn't live off them, so most of the time you had to miss work or spend time away from the family and you weren't properly compensated. I suppose playing rugby at that level was quite a selfish existence really.

I was away from my wife quite a lot, plus, if things didn't go my way on the rugby field I was quite miserable and down about the result – your family sees the worst of you. Nobody can see what you have gone through. As far as everyone else is concerned, it's just a game of rugby. It's only now that I can accept that. At the time, saying that was the biggest insult you could throw at me. Now I realise, when I look back and I'm not involved in it, that it was only a game. But when you are actually involved, when you are living it, you immerse yourself in it: the game, the lifestyle, everything you read is about rugby, everything you learn is about rugby, you pick up the phone and it's all about rugby.

*

The club decided to arrange a testimonial game for me in January of the following year and I played against Bridgend – again! – for a Glenn Webbe Invitation International XV. It was nice of the club to do that for me. Neville Walsh, who was behind The Crawshays, arranged most of it – he was a cracking fella, he was Mr Crawshays. Strictly speaking, you weren't allowed to hold such games at the time as rugby hadn't quite gone professional.

After the game I turned left out of the changing rooms and walked out of the players' entrance to look at the vastness of that old paddy field, the 'Be Wary Field', one last time and I had a quiet moment to myself.

In the clubhouse afterwards, I was presented with an inscribed tankard that still sits in my house. It was good. I had great feedback from Bridgend. I'd only ever played for Bridgend; sure I'd guested for other sides on tour and played in charity games, but they were my only club, and they always will be. I loved the town and I loved the supporters and the club. I still do today. It's such a pity they are struggling for survival at this moment in time, but then again, so many of the old first-class clubs are – and some, such as Maesteg, Glamorgan Wanderers and Penarth are in even deeper trouble. I know you can't live in the past, and Wales are really competitive on the world stage on a regular basis now, but at what price?

*

I didn't know it at the time, but my decision to retire from rugby may have been influenced by a serious illness that could have been terminal. It was only after retiring, when I became noticeably ill, that it was diagnosed but there were signs when I looked back over my final season with Bridgend.

One training session, John Phelps took us on a warm-up run through the town. I was never one for endurance running but I really struggled to complete the run and had to stop and walk. I began to get tired pretty quickly and I just thought, 'this is what happens when you get into your 30s, you just slow down.'

But after retiring I began to notice little clues that something wasn't quite right. I would stop halfway up the stairs and look around and think 'the ceiling needs painting', but I was actually just giving myself a reason to stop and catch my breath. Then I started having to get up five or six times a night to go to the toilet. I was on the road as a rep at the time and I would even have to plan my route around where I knew there would be toilets. Sometimes I would be caught short and would just pull the car up and jump over a fence, absolutely bursting, but when I went to go, virtually nothing came out. I would wake up at night in a pool of sweat. My appetite had gone, I dropped two stone in weight and I was constantly tired.

I eventually went to the doctor and they did some tests. They took blood and a sample out of a gland in my neck, and I was diagnosed as having Hodgkin's Lymphoma, a form of cancer.

They began monitoring me. I had to give blood every week or so, and I was put on medication – they even put me on steroids to try and boost my immune system. It was pretty dreadful. I was losing my appetite, losing weight, getting tired – just thinking, this is my slow decline. The doctors told me to stop training and not to exert myself. In the end I felt like a real victim. I thought, 'This is not how I wanted to finish my days; just fading away.'

I had regular appointments with the doctor but, every time I went, I felt worse leaving the surgery than I did before. So I stopped going. And I stopped taking the medication.

I just decided to start training again. I pushed myself and pushed myself. I didn't have anyone telling me not to do anything, it was just me training. And after training I started to feel hungry. Slowly, after my training sessions, my appetite started to come back. Then slowly, my energy levels started to increase. The more energy I had, the more I trained. And the more I trained, the hungrier I became. And the hungrier I became, the more I ate. I had created a cycle. My weight started to come back and I became a lot more confident about ignoring the doctor's advice, as I began to feel better in myself. It took a while, it wasn't an overnight transformation, but within a year I was back to normal as far as I was concerned. I even returned to the game as a player/coach.

I wouldn't advise anyone else not to take their doctor's advice and stop their treatment, but I would advise everyone not to give up hope – rather, to have the strength of character to believe in themselves. The mind is an amazing thing and you can overcome a lot of things with positive thinking and positive attitudes. I definitely think you should breed positivity. I tell my daughters that they can achieve almost anything they put their minds to. Believe first, achieve second. But you have got to have that fundamental belief.

I never asked whether it was terminal. I wouldn't want to know, but I do know that it was a serious illness and that people had died of it. So the possibility was there and if I had asked the question, my doctor may have given me an answer that I would have found difficult to live with – quite literally.

CHAPTER 13

Life after rugby

THERE'S NO DOUBT that when you have given your life to rugby it can be difficult to adjust when you leave it all behind – it must be the same with all sports. A lot of sportspeople, after the comedown, try to re-evaluate and find a place in today's world for themselves, but it's very difficult to do. It's such a fine line between success and failure, happiness and sadness, love and hate – it's all just on a knife edge.

Dafydd James has fairly recently spoken out about the anxiety and depression he felt after failing to readjust to life after rugby – he even admitted considering taking his own life. I am so proud of him for showing such bravery in speaking out to shed some light on the issue and sincerely hope he is now getting the help and support he needs.

Unfortunately, Dafydd is by no means alone, and my old mate, the BBC Wales rugby pundit Phil Steele, who also grew up in Ely, has also suffered with severe depression, as explained in his brilliant book, *Nerves of Steele*. I take my hat off to anyone who has the courage to speak out on such an important issue and I think the message is slowly getting across.

*

This was brought home to me, all too painfully, when I lost my best friend, Mike Budd, in 2013, aged just 46.

You will recall Buddy was a year younger than me but

when he moved up from youth to senior rugby, he also joined Bridgend. We had first become friends playing for Cardiff & District Youth together; he also played for a smaller, less fashionable club, St Joseph's. We got along really well, he shared the same sense of humour and also liked a good sing-song after games.

He had made the same pact about not joining Cardiff Youth and had also gone on to win a cap with Wales Youth. After seeing how I had enjoyed a successful season with Bridgend, he asked me to do the same thing that Robbie had done for me, put in a word to see if he could join pre-season training the following year. The coaches said they would love to see him, so he came along and became a permanent fixture.

He used to play a lot of sevens and was a fantastic sevens player. He had good pace and was a heavy boy with great hands. He was also a tremendous 15-a-side player, such an athlete, but the fact that he used to get in where it hurts was probably to his detriment. He was such an unselfish, team player – he was always the players' player of the match. A lot of the things he did were unglamorous and went unseen, which meant he was overlooked by the Welsh selectors for far too long.

He always had this big grin on his face, he would smile all the time. You would be standing by the bar after the game and Buddy would come in, tap you on your left shoulder and, of course, when you turned around, he would be standing on your right-hand side doing that silent laugh of his. It got to the stage where he would tap you on the shoulder and you would automatically look the opposite way. He was always the life and soul of the party and on away trips he would be the one pulling the players together with lots stupid of jokes and the stupidest of pranks... he was impossible not to like or to feel for.

We had no idea what was behind that smile of his – I know now that it was a case of the tears of a clown; he was just really hurting behind that whole exterior.

Buddy often pops up in lists of 'best players never to play for

Wales' but he did play for Wales. He played against Canada in Edmonton for Wales in 1989, at a time when Canada weren't considered a top-tier nation so it was under the banner of Wales B. However, the fixture was later upgraded and a lot of players were awarded retrospective caps. Sadly he wasn't around to collect his in person.

I couldn't believe it when I heard he had passed away. This is how poignant it was.

There was a stage when there was a lot of doom and gloom around the Bridgend area as there were a number of youngsters who had taken their own lives. There was a big, black cloud hanging over the whole of the town – not helped by the media writing sensationalistic stories on the seemingly abnormal number of young deaths with talk of suicide cults.

As a result, a few of us players decided to get together and see whether there was something that we could do for the place – it was instigated by Buddy. Somewhat poignantly, we had all gathered for Colin Hillman's funeral, and we said there must be something that we could do. It was Buddy who said, "We're going to have a meeting at the club and everyone, no matter what you are doing, has to be there. You have to turn up."

The date came along and we were all there waiting for Buddy. We tried ringing him but there was no answer – he didn't turn up. We were all cursing him saying, "He's the one who arranged all this and he didn't even turn up to his own meeting." Little did we know that he had just been going through some really ridiculous times. We found out how bad things were for him a few weeks later... that's when we heard the news.

I heard it on the radio. I just fell over, I fell to the floor and cried like a baby. It was absolutely devastating. I just couldn't believe it. I was ringing everyone but their phones were engaged – everyone must have been trying to ring each other. I was choked. We were just talking about the very thing that he did. There had been a lack of understanding, I remember saying how cowardly it must be for someone to take their own life.

These kids hadn't considered others, they were being selfish, it's the people who they left behind who really suffered. I really didn't understand the issues that they were going through.

Personally, I've changed my mind about what I previously thought about suicide. If you have never experienced the darkness, you would think along those lines. It's not until it's explained to you from their point of view that you begin to see where they are coming from. It must be awful – there's nothing you can do, there's so many chemical imbalances that make you go that way, you can't just pull yourself together like people tell you to. It's a real, deep-rooted condition.

I know that Buddy had a hell of a lot of work on. When I spoke to his wife, she said he would just not speak about things. She wanted him to seek out medical help and get checked out properly but he refused. He just locked himself away and wouldn't talk. She said that when he was with his friends he was OK, but he was just hiding it all. Behind closed doors he must have been really struggling.

If any good can come out of it all then it's another chance to get the message out there that if you are struggling, then you really should talk to somebody about it. I realise now that communication is important. I always say that the best teams will beat the best players because they share the workload but that also works if you have issues or problems or if you can't deal with something. A lot of the time when you are alone, that's where the demons are.

When you don't share your thoughts, you have nobody that can contradict your negative thoughts, and so they can grow. The more you are alone the more you think about your problems, and they grow. If you are contemplating suicide, the idea of it is virtually a comfort and that is what you are looking for. All of your pain can stop. All of your doubt can stop. You think you are just becoming a burden on everybody. You are worthless and you will be helping everybody out by taking yourself out of the equation. It's an awful way to think about yourself. Because you don't share and you think people won't understand, you would rather shy away and take comfort in your negative thoughts. You really think because you feel so bad about yourself, you are doing everyone a favour. But it is not the case.

If this is you, then please talk to somebody.

*

As I have said, when you stop playing there's a massive adjustment you have to make. When you are playing rugby, especially at a high level, you almost spend more time with the people you play with than you do with your family. It's fundamentally who you are. So, once the game stops, you stop being who you were. When you're not playing any more, you are somebody else. A lot of the time players don't have anything outside of the game. Once they stop being who they are, it's very difficult to fill that void and there's an emptiness there. You have to substitute it with something even if it's just gradually. A lot of players go into coaching or get involved in the rugby environment of their local clubs. You can't just stop. You almost have to wean yourself off the game and find a substitute.

When I finished playing there was a bit of a void there and so I did my Level Two WRU coaching course and took up an offer to coach Tondu for a while. I quite enjoyed it, although a lot of the time it was a case of, "This is the last time I'm going to show you", and then take the tracksuit off and go on the field and have a run. They were playing some good stuff for a lower league side.

I had an ulterior motive for taking up an offer to coach Tondu, however, as the club had let me down on a business deal as far as I was concerned. I was selling uPVC windows and Tondu bought the town's old fire station and converted it into a clubhouse. They came to me for a quote to replace the old windows and told me I had the job. I had the windows made – they cost a lot of money – and when I went to fit them I found that the job had already been done by somebody else without telling me. I was stuck with a factory full of windows that I couldn't do anything with – they had been made to measure. There was nowhere I could go.

So, when the offer to coach there came, I told a third party that I wouldn't look sideways at Tondu again but he just said, "Look, the best way to get back at them is from the inside."

He said, "Just think of the money you could be on for playing and coaching." He got my attention because I was absolutely devastated. I didn't have a great deal of money, virtually everything I had had gone into the windows, and they had completely disowned the fact that they had given me the job. I had paid for everything up front and hadn't even taken a deposit from them because the club was struggling, and then someone came along and undercut me and they went with it.

So, I got on board with them and did a lot with their social activities. Then Tondu were drawn in the Cup against Swansea. It was one of the biggest games in the club's history. I was involved in corporate hospitality and so I said to the club that there was quite a lot of money to be made. I spoke to a few celebrities who did after-dinner speaking and arranged for a marquee to be put up next to the ground and sold a lot of tables to local businesses, spoke to a couple of breweries and arranged for sponsorship. I made posters and the tickets and even sold the tickets. It was just a fantastic day.

I had a separate account set up and everything which I had generated went into that with me as the trustee. A couple of weeks after the game the club came to me and said, "That was fantastic what you did there Glenn, we never thought we would be able to do anything like this. You have given us the foresight and we are going to take this forward. How much did we actually generate?" It was around what I had lost.

Then they asked, "What do we do now? How do we divide this money up?"

I said, "We don't."

"What?"

"I said we don't. I'm keeping all of it."

They said, "What?"

I said, "I did all the work, I sold all the tickets. I put it all together." Then I added, "Remember those f****** windows? I'm keeping it."

I felt that I was owed it. They must have realised that I was right as I had another season with Tondu and helped them get promotion – but they didn't let me organise a celebration dinner!

*

As far as work was concerned, I was working all along while playing rugby, selling double glazing. I remember our prop and later forwards coach, Ian Stephens, used to always say, "Here comes Webbe's wonky windows!" I used to have a slogan of my own, "Where there's a window, there's a Webbe! From windows to doors, to ceilings to floors."

A couple of years after retiring I switched to finance, selling home mortgages and finance to home improvement companies. Then I started with this big kitchen company, working on their finance side helping customers with payment plans. One day the manager suggested I go on one of their kitchen training courses as it might make my finance sales pitches more relevant. I must have a creative streak in me because I quite enjoyed it.

Not long after, one of the kitchen designers was off sick and there was a customer waiting and I was asked to fill in. I will never forget, it was a Mrs Jones, up in Ebbw Vale, and she had her heart set on this blue kitchen with a maple wood worktop. She loved it and I made the sale. It cost her £4,000 and I received £400 in commission – just for a night's work. After that I began selling kitchens in the evenings and finance in the day. Money was coming in left, right and centre, but something had to give because I was working myself to a standstill.

I decided to focus on selling kitchens and eventually became a manager. My job was to make sure that the business was running smoothly and, now and then, I would cherry-pick the leads and pop in on the way home and sell a kitchen. Then, one day, I called on this lovely old lady in Fairwater. She was talking about her only son being grown up and living away and that she never had many visitors, it was just her alone with her dog. We discussed a kitchen and she wanted to buy it. The cost came to £6,000 but I knew that I could get it fitted for around £150 and the units would only be £400, so I said, "I'll speak to you on Monday."

"I really do want it," she said. "I'm not wasting your time."

"I know," I said. "I'll work something out for you." She was a lovely woman and I didn't want her spending all that money on a kitchen. I had become friendly with the suppliers and the fitters and was well aware of the cost price of kitchens and what we sold them for – there was an astronomical profit being made. So I spoke to the boys about fitting it as a hobble over a weekend and I looked into buying the units myself at trade cost.

I called her on the Monday and she said, "Can I give you the deposit?"

I said, "I can get a kitchen for you but it will be much cheaper."

She replied, "No, I want the one you showed me."

"Don't worry, it will be the same kitchen."

She said, "I don't want this conversation to go any further." And she just hung up on me.

Around an hour later I had a phone call from the owner of the company, who was based in London. He said, "Glenn, I need to speak to you. Stay in the office." Three hours later he had driven down the M4 all that way just to see me.

"You've been selling company leads," he said. "You either leave now or we will sack you."

I tried to explain myself but I had nowhere to go. That lovely old lady had grassed me up. I left there and then, thinking to myself, 'You just can't help some people.'

Looking at it now, she may have done me the biggest favour of them all because after that I decided to set up on my own. Things have grown and grown and today I have the Kitchen Bureau, off Penarth Road in Cardiff, with the largest kitchen showroom in Wales.

I put a large part of my success in business down to what I learnt during my rugby career. I really think that rugby has given me one hell of an education. You would look at a player, and by their size and weight you would be able to say what position they were – that's not the case today as they are all huge, apart from most scrum-halves – and there would be 15 people on the field. They would also all have different qualities and attributes but they would all have a common goal: to win the game. It all came down to teamwork. The team was paramount. Everyone was playing for the team and working for the team. It's the exact same principle when you run your own business – you have got to get your team right.

You may think that you can do it on your own but you can't succeed without the backing and support of the people around you. That's what I've taken from rugby, the team ethic.

CHAPTER 14

Last word

I NEVER DID join Cardiff and I'm proud to say that I only ever played for one senior club. I did come close on one or two occasions, mind you. First when Robbie joined Cardiff, and later when Mike Budd eventually went the same way. I really didn't want him to go. Obviously, I wouldn't have followed him just because he went – you have to think about yourself – but his going did make me really think about the position that I was in. Perhaps I needed a change, but I was still a first-choice player at Bridgend at that time and I had also been capped.

I went to a Bridgend former players' reunion recently and I looked at the bar and there were players at one end from the Eighties, and they went all the way along to players from the late Nineties, who didn't really know the other group, and I thought, 'There's my career right there!' It seemed to merge into one big season and I was the common denominator between them all! Bridgend was the only club I ever played for, and I wouldn't have it any other way.

*

When I look back, I am grateful for everything Bridgend did for me but I have also never forgotten Canton RFC, another club that is close to my heart. There are still a lot of people down there who I know and love. When I was playing for Bridgend and was out injured, I would try to go down and watch Canton, and if I was on the way back from injury I would play for them beforehand. I believe my picture still hangs in the clubhouse; I don't think they have turned it around just yet!

*

I've never thought of myself as a great player and I don't think I've ever really been ambitious, although I have always wanted to beat the man next to me. In any environment I wanted to be as good as I could be and I finally did what my teachers advised, and tried harder. I'm individually competitive but there was never a pathway or goal as far as rugby was concerned. I never looked up to an icon or studied someone's game or wished or hoped or prayed for anything really – things just seemed to happen. I was at a certain place at a certain time and took my opportunity. I really liked rugby but it wasn't the actual game, it was the friendships that kept me in the game.

Internationally, I only had ten caps but was on the bench five times and in this day and age I would almost certainly have come on to add to the total. But I've done more than most people – not many people can say they've had one cap for Wales, never mind ten and played in a Rugby World Cup. However, once you get one cap, you want two. Once you get two you want ten, and once you get ten you just want to be a permanent fixture. But as Wayne Hall tells people, "It's better to be a has-been than a never-was."

I'm grateful for the game of rugby. Without it I wouldn't be the person I am. I really do think rugby is a religion in itself, it brings people together, keeps you grounded... and there's also lots of singing!

Hallelujah and Amen to that.

Friends and fans

Glenn was a regular with Bridgend when I first joined Swansea. He was very, very quick and always amongst the top three or four wingers in Welsh rugby during his era and deserved his chance with Wales when he got it.

He was an incredibly strong player but used his pace more than anything to beat players – he had the ability to glide around people. He was a tremendous try-scorer for Bridgend for many years and one of the most talented wingers of his generation.

Webby is genuinely a great guy, a real character and someone you enjoyed being with both on and off the field. I have been on several tours with him and to the Rugby World Cup in 1987. I will never forget Webby leading us in playing drinking games with the crew of a cable-laying ship when we were in Fiji – I woke up on the toilet to discover my teammates gone and the ship about to embark on its next tour of duty somewhere!

Robert Jones – Swansea, Wales and British & Irish Lions

During my time with both Neath and Wales, Glenn was undoubtedly one of the most charismatic players in the Welsh arena, not only because of his phenomenal capabilities on the field, but also because of his lively presence off it.

He scored numerous tries during his career, but one in particular stands out for me and that was the try he scored for Wales when we played Tonga in the inaugural Rugby World

Cup in 1987. It stood out not only because he carved his way around the ferocious Tongan defence but, more impressively, because he was severely concussed following a head-high tackle earlier in the match. Sadly, having helped Wales secure the victory, the ferocity of the tackle and the impact on Glenn was such that his condition was deemed bad enough by the medical staff for him to be sent home and his World Cup was over.

The other thing that stands out was his physique, something he has managed to maintain despite hanging up his boots over 20 years ago, and while many of his peers have succumbed to age and the lure of socialising.

Paul Thorburn – Neath and Wales

Glennfield Webbe and I are good friends. We met at a Cardiff & District Youth rugby trial at Glamorgan Wanderers RFC back in the 1980–81 season. Glenn started in the Red XV and remained there throughout while I progressed from the White XV into the Red XV for the final game of the season. I could see how quick and powerful Glenn was and tried to get the ball to him as often as I could. I think he liked me for that, as wingers can sometimes be frustrated with a lack of opportunities but on this occasion Glenn showed everyone what he could do and we were both lucky enough to make the starting line-up for all of Cardiff & District's fixtures that season (when we were undefeated) before both progressing into the Wales Youth team.

That Cardiff & District Youth team bonded well as a group and Glenn should take most of the credit for this, as he was undoubtedly the 'life and soul'. The players were drawn to him as he was not only an outstanding rugby player but he could sing and knew all the best rugby songs, he could tell a good story, a hysterical joke and even do close-up magic. He taught me all his magic tricks and I still use them today, usually when

I'm half-cut down the pub or to entertain my six-year-old twins!

Whenever Cardiff & District Youth played away matches, the team bus had a set route to drop the players off at various points closer to their homes, but more often than not, most of the squad stayed on the bus and got off in Ely (where Glenn lived) where we all followed him to the nearest pub to carry on the banter.

Glenn and I both went on to be capped at senior level and we spent the best part of ten years together in various Wales squads, and we were lucky enough to go on tour and play at the Rugby World Cup. Nothing ever really changed as Glenn would be immensely popular with all the senior squad and arranged all the off-field entertainment.

Unfortunately for Glenn, he was a right wing vying for the same starting position as the brilliantly talented Ieuan Evans. If Evans hadn't been around, Glenn would probably have been selected for the British & Irish Lions and won many more full caps.

One story I always remember involved former coach Ron Waldron's announcement to the players that Ieuan Evans would be his first captain under his command. He said, "I've just announced to the press that Ieuan is captain of Wales. Now where's Webbe? Stand up Webbe! Now you play for Bridgend on the right wing but Ieuan is also a right wing and as captain of his country he is the first name on the team sheet. So what I'd advise you to do, Webbe, is go back to Bridgend and ask them for more game time on the left wing."

So standing there, in among all the players, Glenn looked at Ron, gripped his Wales tracksuit top in the region of his heart and replied, "Ron, I will play anywhere for you and for my country; even if you selected me to play for Wales as a tighthead prop, I'd do it for you Ron... but I'd play it like a right winger!" And he sat back down.

Glenn and I have been friends all along. He remains the 'life and soul' and I must confess to still getting a little excited when

I'm dressing up for some function in the knowledge Glennfield Webbe is going to be there!

Mark Ring – Cardiff and Wales

I have known my fellow 'Ely Boy' Glenn since I was about ten years old. He was a talented athlete and fabulous rugby player but, more importantly, he is an outstanding human being who has never forgotten his roots.

His sense of fun and humour are legendary and this makes him great company in any situation.

I'll never forget his quip after he returned from the Wales Youth tour of South Africa in 1980 which put the evil of that country's abhorrent apartheid system firmly in its place:

"They were so good to me those South Africans – they gave me a bus, hotel and cinema all to myself!"

That was typical of Glenn's attitude never to be cowed by anyone or anything and all infused with his typical mischievous wit.

You've done Ely proud Glenn, and it's a privilege to know you.

Phil Steele – Newport and BBC Wales rugby broadcaster

Glenn Webbe is a Bridgend RFC legend. We all remember the fashion, the hairstyles and the famous gloves, although his major characteristic was his one-club career loyalty. He was a supporters' favourite, lightning-quick, strong in the tackle, scoring tries for fun. He was selected just out of youth to face the touring Wallabies in 1981 and will never be forgotten.

Wayne Barrington – Mr Bridgend,
a Ravens supporter for more than 50 years

You meet a lot of people in rugby and sport but Webby is very special. He's a great guy, a great friend. What a great socialiser, always full of jokes, just a great guy to have around.

I was the reason that he started wearing gloves, because he couldn't catch the ball! We had some great duels playing for Pontypool and Bridgend over the years. I used to say to him, before putting a box-kick up, "It's coming Webby!" And he would reply, "Bring it on."

We played a lot sevens together and won a lot of tournaments. What stands out is the time he faced David Trick, the Bath and England wing, who was said to be one of the fastest players in English rugby. I was winding Webby up saying that Trick was the fastest thing on two legs and that he wouldn't be able to live with his pace.

He came face to face with him in the semi-finals and we were winning, something like 30–10, and the referee said it was the last play. Being captain, I told the boys not to bother making a tackle, just save their energy for the final. I kicked long and Trick caught the ball and started running – we all stood still, apart from Webby! He sprinted after Trick and caught him from behind just before the line.

I asked him what he was doing, and he said, "He's not that quick!"

David Bishop – Pontypool and Wales

I first came across Glenn in the final trial for Welsh Youth in 1980. I remember him as this magnificent human specimen who could have represented Wales in athletics in the 200m. Fortunately, we both got selected for the Welsh Youth side that toured South Africa that year, where I got to know him really well and our friendship has remained until this day.

I remember him teaching me many rugby songs on that tour, in particular 'Running Bear', which I will never forget. Glenn became an icon on that tour as it was during the apartheid era and all the black South Africans supported us!

I was so pleased when Glenn finally represented Wales on the tour to the South Sea Islands in 1986 before going on to the Rugby World Cup.

I wish him and his family all the best for the future.

Bleddyn Bowen – former Wales captain

I first came across Glenn when he was 18 and we were both in youth rugby. He played against us down in Stradey and he scored a few tries. He was always outstanding, quick, powerful and elusive. He had it all. I knew then that he was going to make it.

He was a tremendous player, a great winger, he was definitely of international class and his call to the senior team, when it finally came, was thoroughly deserved.

And it was typical of Glenn to make himself stand out more by wearing those gloves!

When I first saw them, I thought to myself, 'What is he doing?' But then again, some nights, he must have been freezing out on the wing down the Brewery Field and up in places like Eugene Cross Park. On the other hand, he wore them out in Tonga, so it couldn't have been because he was cold!

He scored a hat-trick against Tonga in the World Cup but couldn't remember anything about it because he was concussed. I came on as a sub in that game and I can remember him just wandering about. There were a lot of high shots going around. When I came on, one of their players was looking at me and making a gesture that he was going to slit my throat. It was just weird.

Off the field Glenn is a brilliant laugh, he is such a character. He has a dry Cardiff wit, is sarcastic and takes the mick out of himself. He is brilliant company. There's never a dull moment with Glenn. He's just a great character, really funny – in the 1987 Rugby World Cup we made him and Ring social managers.

If you're ever on tour he's the one you want around.

Jonathan Davies – Neath, Llanelli and Wales

Glenn gave Bridgend RFC and myself personally a career of wearing the blue and white. EVERY club wanted him at his peak but he stayed with us. His loyalty and popularity will remain with me forever!

Derrick King – Bridgend chairman

Acknowledgments

I WOULD LIKE to thank Geraint Thomas for convincing me that I had a story to tell and Y Lolfa for helping him make this book a reality. Also a special word of thanks to all the former players, Rob Howley in particular, who took time to write such kind words about this boy from Ely. And lastly, but by no means least, all the Bridgend supporters, led by superfan Wayne Barrington, who cheered me on all the years – it was an honour to wear the blue and white.

Also from Y Lolfa:

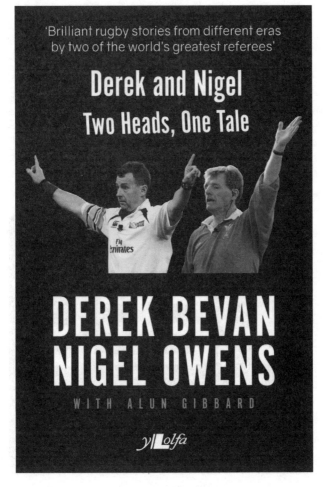

'Brilliant rugby stories from different eras
by two of the world's greatest referees'

Derek and Nigel
Two Heads, One Tale

DEREK BEVAN
NIGEL OWENS

WITH ALUN GIBBARD

y Lolfa

£7.99

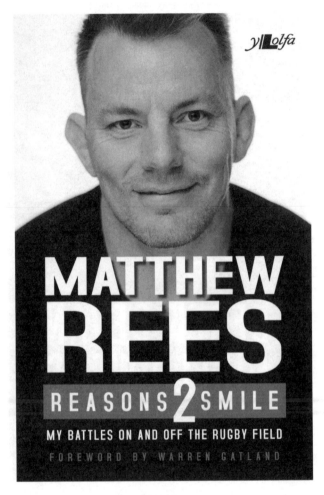

yLolfa

MATTHEW REES

REASONS 2 SMILE

MY BATTLES ON AND OFF THE RUGBY FIELD

FOREWORD BY WARREN GATLAND

£9.99

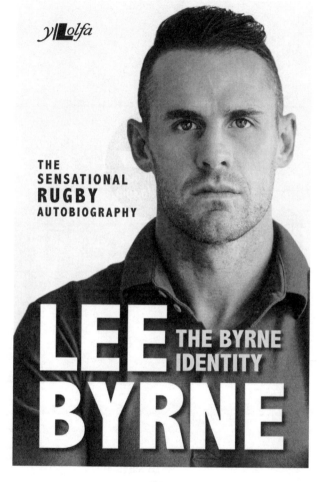

y Lolfa

THE
SENSATIONAL
RUGBY
AUTOBIOGRAPHY

LEE THE BYRNE
IDENTITY

BYRNE

£9.99

03/2020.